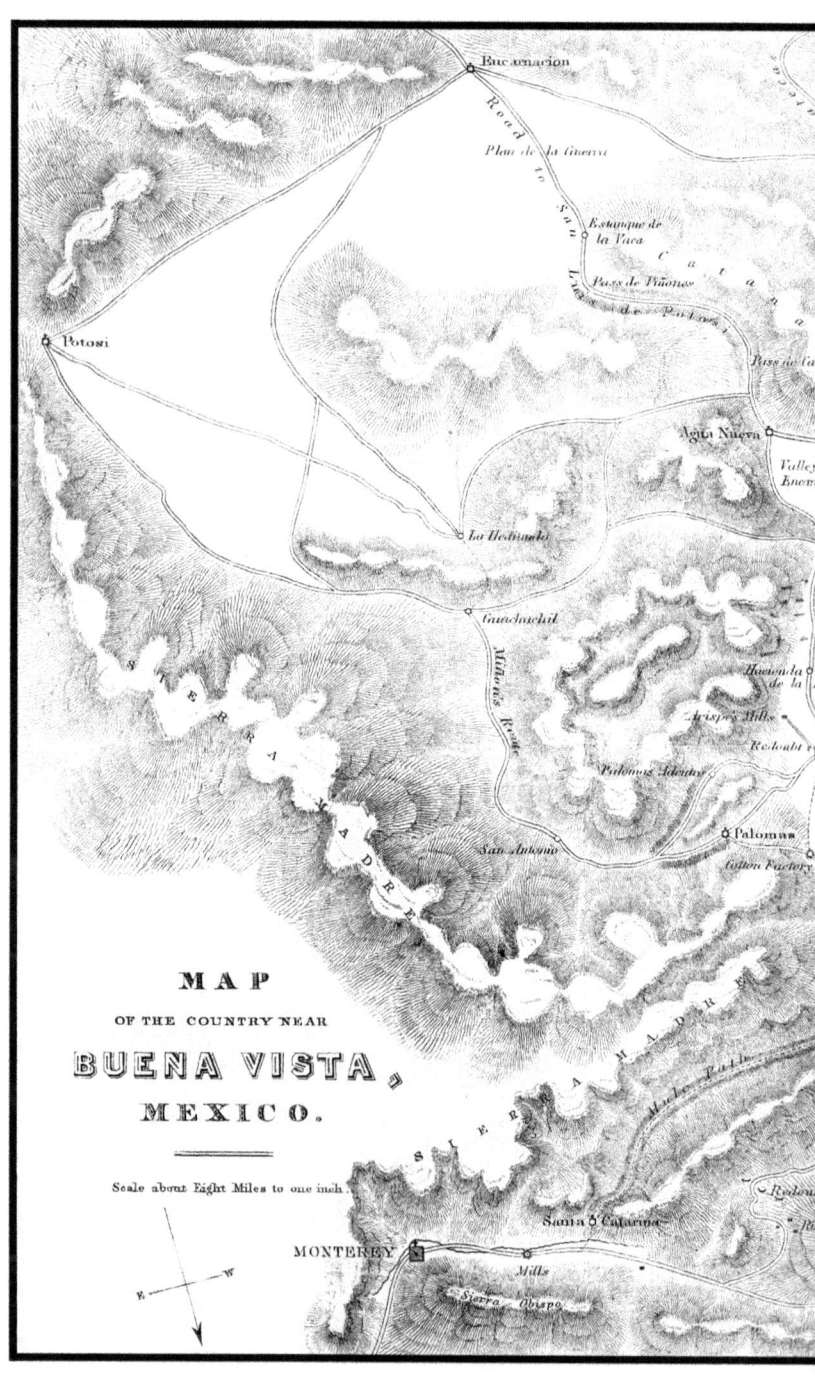

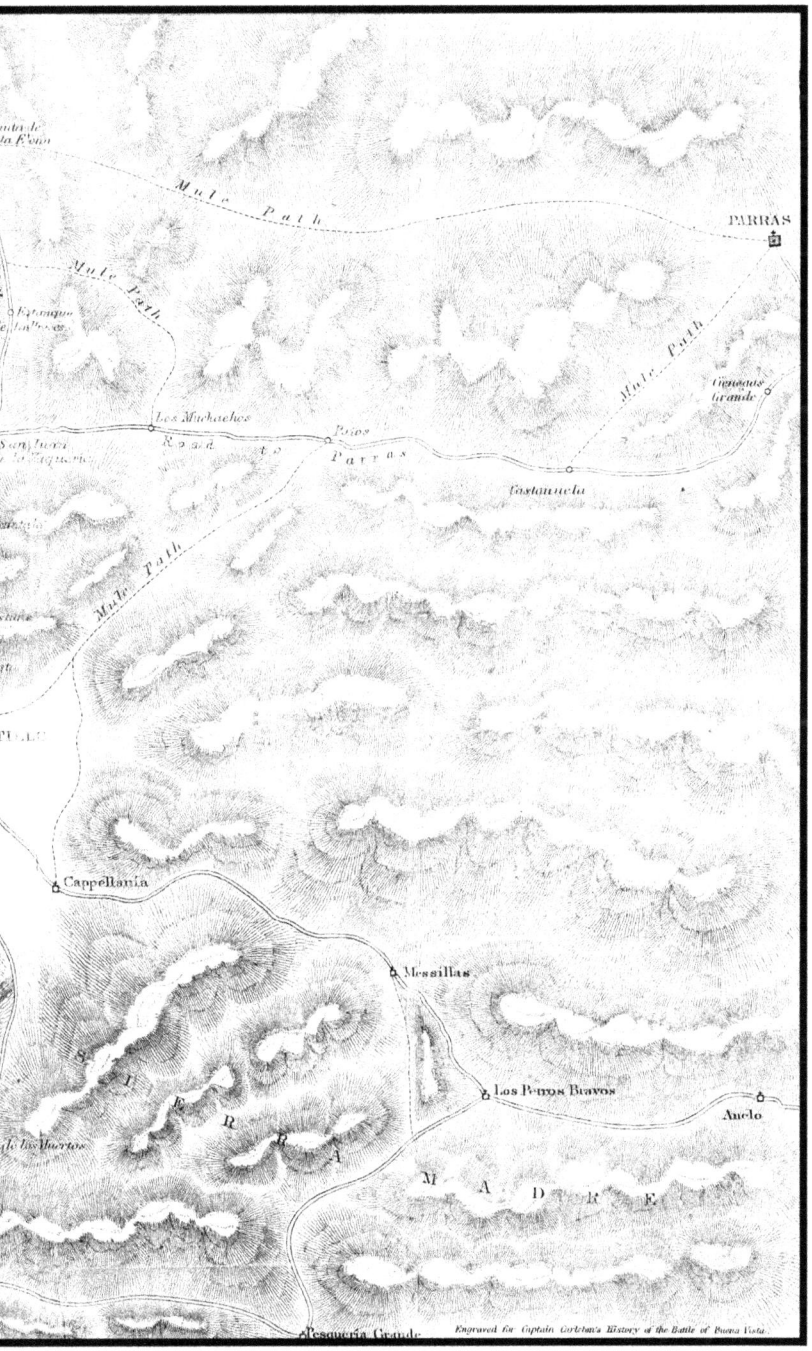

THE BATTLE OF BUENA VISTA,

WITH

THE OPERATIONS

OF THE

"ARMY OF OCCUPATION"

FOR ONE MONTH.

BY

JAMES HENRY CARLETON,

CAPTAIN IN THE FIRST REGIMENT OF DRAGOONS.

The Naval & Military Prees Ltd.

Published by

The Naval & Military Press Ltd
Unit 5 Riverside, Brambleside
Bellbrook Industrial Estate
Uckfield, East Sussex
TN22 1QQ England

Tel: +44 (0)1825 749494

www.naval-military-press.com
www.nmarchive.com

*In reprinting in facsimile from the original, any imperfections are inevitably reproduced
and the quality may fall short of modern type and cartographic standards.*

TO

MAJOR-GENERAL ZACHARY TAYLOR

THIS ACCOUNT OF

THE BATTLE OF BUENA VISTA

IS RESPECTFULLY

INSCRIBED.

PREFACE.

It is due to those who are immediately interested in the accuracy of the following account, as well as to the historian who may hereafter consult it, to state what were the opportunities of the writer for knowing the truth.

For two months before the battle of Buena Vista, he was stationed at or near the ground on which it was fought; and, during this time, he was led, with others, to remark its strength as a military position.

In the battle itself, the nature of the service he was called on to perform as commander of a company of dragoons, afforded opportunities of deliberate observation in many different parts of the scene, and enabled him sometimes to take notes of what was going on around him.

For no less than eight months afterward, he was encamped on the same spot, and had the best opportunities of conferring with the different officers engaged, and of observing accurately the various localities.

Hence arose his purpose of attempting a minute description of the battle, — a purpose he began at once to execute under circumstances which seemed to invite him to the task, convinced as he was, that what had formed so interesting a part of his own experience and observation, would be regarded hereafter as one of the important events in the military history of the country.

With all that fell under his personal notice, or was derived from minute inquiries of other officers immediately after the battle, he has combined the substance of what appeared in the official reports of both parties. To avoid doing injustice to the Mexicans, their reports are generally quoted at the foot of the page.

To Brevet Brigadier-General Churchill, Inspector-General of the Army, he is indebted for the minute report of the killed and wounded, which is inserted in the

Appendix. Brevet Captain Sitgreaves, of the Corps of Topographical Engineers, has kindly furnished him with a Plan of the battle-ground, which was drawn leisurely from careful measurements, and may be relied upon as scientifically correct.

The Map of the surrounding country has been sketched from notes made on the spot, and is sufficiently exact to give an idea of the different routes and positions having any relation to the battle.

In the Appendix are given, beside the documents referred to in the text, several others, which seemed pertinent to the general subject of the book.

With this statement of his opportunities of knowing, and of his inducements to describe, the details of the Battle of Buena Vista, the writer presents his narrative to the public, claiming for it only the consideration due to the fidelity and candor with which he has attempted to compose it.

J. H. C.

Boston, July 4, 1848.

SPREAD I

SPREAD III

PLAN
OF THE
BATTLE OF BUENA VISTA
FOUGHT
February 22nd & 23rd
1847.

Drawn by Brevet-Captain Lorenzo Sitgreaves.
U.S.T.E.

LEGEND

Position of General Taylor during the battle of the 23rd of February.

A. Hacienda San Juan de la Buena Vista.
B. La Angostura.
C. Deep gullies to the right La Angostura.
D. The highland connecting La Angostura.
   with the Plateau.
E. The Plateau.
F. The ravine in rear of the Plateau.
G. The broad ravine in front of the Plateau.
H. The Encampment.
I. The elevated ridge between the first position of the enemy and that of the Americans.
J. The slope of the mountain to the left of the Plateau occupied by Ampudia.
K. The slope of the mountain occupied by the American Riflemen.
L. Position of Lieutenant O'Brienn's section of Artillery & the 2nd Indiana regiment at day break on the 23rd of Feb^y.
M. The Enemy's 8-pounder Battery.
N. Captain Bragg's Battery and the 2nd Kentucky Volunteers.
O. First gorge.
P. Second gorge.
Q. Third gorge.
R. 2nd Illinois Volunteers.
S. Two pieces of Captain Sherman's Battery.
T. Two companies 1st Dragoons.
U. Mc. Culloch's Texan company.
V. Colonel Lane's 3rd Indiana Volunteers.
W. Arkansas and Kentucky regiments Mounted Volnteers.
X. First Column of attack under General Mora y Villanil.
Y. General Lombardim's division.
Z. General Pacheco's division

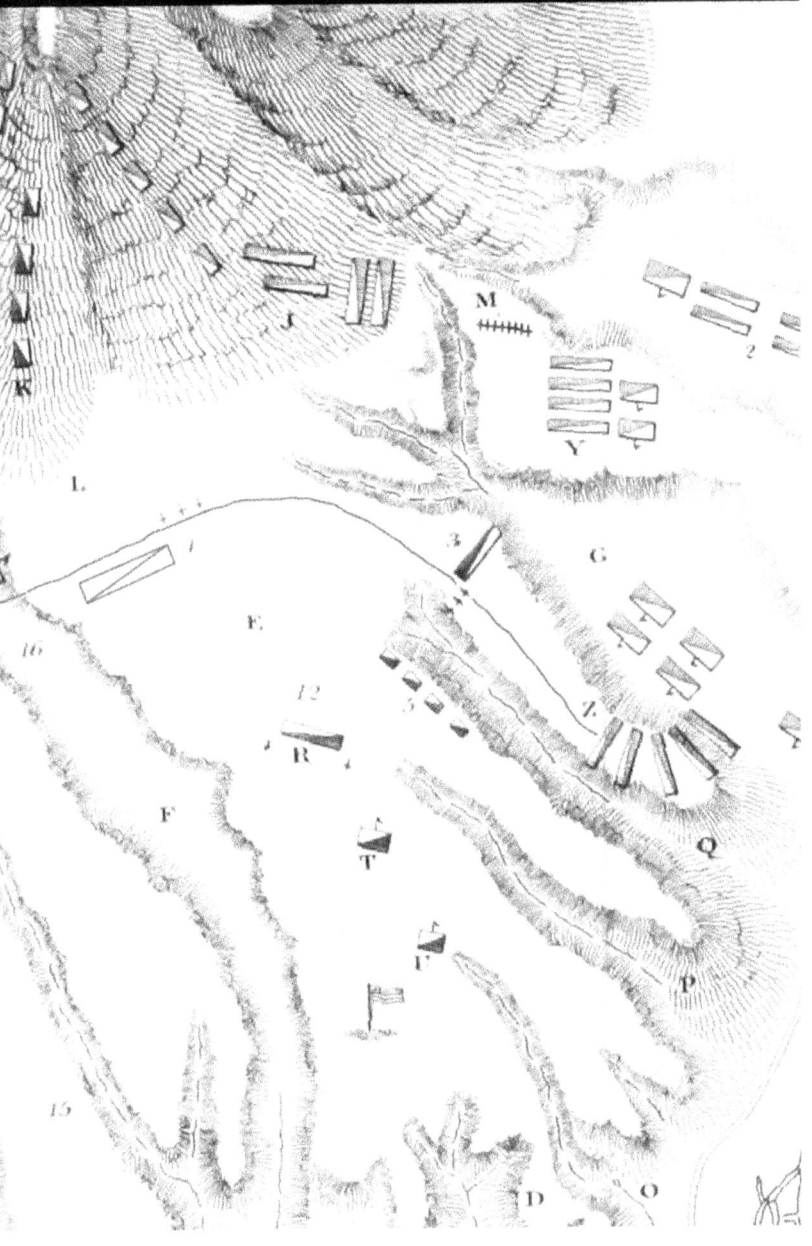

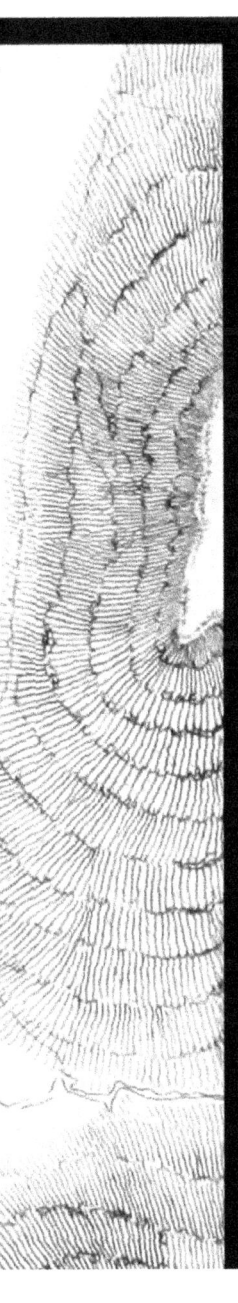

LEGEND

Position of General Taylor during the battle of the 23rd of February.

A. Hacienda San Juan de la Buena Vista.

B. La Angostura.

C. Deep gullies to the right La Angostura.

D. The highland connecting La Angostura. with the Plateau.

E. The Plateau.

F. The ravine in rear of the Plateau.

G The broad ravine in front of the Plateau.

H. The Encampment.

I. The elevatedridge between the first position of the enemy and that of the Americans.

J. The slope of the mountain to the left of the Plateau occupied by Ampudia.

K. The slope of the mountain occupied by the American Riflemen.

L. Position of Lieutenant O'Brienn's sec-

PLAN
OF THE
BATTLE OF BUENA VISTA,
FOUGHT
February 22nd & 23rd
1847.

Drawn by Brevet Captain Lorenzo Sitgreaves,
U. S. T. E.

Engraved for Captain Carleton's History of the Battle of Buena Vista.

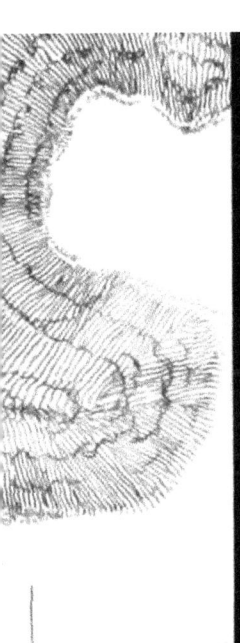

tion of Artillery & the 2nd Indiana regiment at day break on the 23rd of Feb^y.

M. The Enemy's 8-pounder Battery.

N. Captain Bragg's Battery and the 2nd Kentucky Volunteers.

O. First gorge.

P. Second gorge.

Q. Third gorge.

R. 2nd Illinois Volunteers.

S. Two pieces of Captain Sherman's Battery.

T. Two companies 1st Dragoons.

U. Mc. Culloch's Texan company.

V. Colonel Lane's 3rd Indiana Volunteers.

W. Arkansas and Kentucky regiments Mounted Volnteers.

X. First Column of attack under General Mora y Villanil.

Y. General Lombardim's division.

Z. General Pacheco's division

THE

BATTLE OF BUENA VISTA.

THE Battle of Buena Vista has now become the property of the Past. In our country's history, it stands beside that of Trenton, Saratoga, Yorktown, Niagara, and New Orleans; but in many respects it much surpasses them all. Of the numerous triumphs of our arms, it is by far the greatest; as a proof of American valor, it shines forth immeasurably the most glorious. That every individual may clearly understand how it was fought, and how won, nothing more is necessary than a simple array of the facts, which constituted the elements, and characterized the movements, of the two armies on that occasion; which determined the various phases of their protracted conflict; and which finally secured the grand result, — a magnificent victory of the one over the other.

It is the purpose of the following narrative

to set forth, as completely as possible, those facts in their true light; to speak impartially of both sides; in fine, to pass before the eye of the reader a panorama of the battle, with no other than its own fearful embellishments.

It was, without doubt, the original purpose of General Taylor, in the event of Santa Anna's marching from San Luis de Potosi to attack him, to offer battle at Agua Nueva, a hacienda twenty miles south of Saltillo, near which place he was then encamped. Accordingly, by the 10th of February, he had moved all his troops thither with the exception of Captain Webster's Battery of two 24-pounder howitzers,—which was left to occupy a redoubt that our forces had erected on an eminence commanding the approaches to the city,—and a small battalion of riflemen, under Major Warren, of the First Regiment of Illinois Volunteers, to protect the dépôt of ammunition and provisions still remaining behind.

It was necessary to select some place for an encampment, where the ground would be sufficiently extensive and otherwise suitable for the instruction of the troops; where wood and water would be convenient; and where, if circumstances should require it, a battle might be fought to good advantage. Agua Nueva possessed all these requisites in a greater degree than any other place within a hundred miles of Saltillo. Opposed to some strong reasons against it, as a position for battle, there were many in its favor. The enemy, in advancing upon the direct and great thoroughfare from San Luis de Potosí, had necessarily to approach by the hacienda La Encarnacion. Thence to Agua Nueva, it was thirty-five miles through a desert; a long and fatiguing march for any species of troops, but particularly for artillery and infantry, and without one drop of water for the whole distance, — the first to be found being entirely in our possession. Therefore, by maintaining that place, General Taylor would have the advantage of the enemy's disarray from a forced march, of his consequent fatigue, and, more than all, of the unfitness of his men and animals, from long-continued thirst, for immediate battle; while, on the contrary, his own troops would be perfectly fresh, and prepared at all points to receive him. Besides, unless some spot should be chosen still farther in advance, it was better, when this was once occupied, to maintain it if possible, than to select one in the rear; because the fact of retiring on the approach of an enemy, even for a better position, would be calculated to exert a moral effect upon raw troops greatly to be dreaded, as it would cause them to lose confidence not only in their own strength, but in the sagacity, firmness, and hopes of their leader, and, on the other hand, would serve to inspire their antagonists with a more exalted idea of their own prowess.

These reasons for considering this spot as a very good one for a battle-ground were chiefly dependent on the supposition, that Santa Anna, if he came at all, would approach the Americans, encamped upon it, from La Encarnacion, by the direct road. Agua Nueva is situated at the southern extremity of the beautiful valley of La Encantada; and there were two other routes, by which, with great exertions, he might enter it. On one, he could march to the right, by La Hedionda, and thereby gain Buena Vista in our rear; and, on the other, he could pass to the left, by La Punta de Santa Elena, so as to attain the hacienda San Juan de la Vaquería, which would likewise enable him to get possession of the road to Saltillo, and oblige our army to fight under the disadvantage of having its communication entirely cut off. These were contingencies, and the only ones, which would render a change of position imperative. As a last resort, therefore, to be determined upon and adopted according to the dispositions of the enemy, his strength, the description of his forces, and the manner of his approach, General Taylor had it in his power to move back, and take another ground, which, as early as the December previous, General Wool had selected* as a most excellent one for battle, and which, under certain circumstances, would be greatly superior to that which the army then occupied. This latter point was the Pass of BUENA VISTA, six miles in front of Saltillo, and fourteen in rear of Agua Nueva.

The Pass of Buena Vista breaks through a chain of lofty mountains, which, running from east to west, divides the valley north of Saltillo from the more elevated one of La Encantada. It varies in width from a mile and a half to four miles; having the rancho of La Encantada at its southern and narrowest ex-

---
* See Appendix, B.

tremity, at the point where it debouches upon the plain in the valley of that name, and, at its northern extremity, the city of Saltillo, built immediately upon the side of the declivity by which it abruptly terminates, as with a step, or *leap*, to the valley below the town. From La Encantada a small stream of water finds its way through the Pass to Saltillo, and, although it keeps much nearer to the mountains on the western side, still affords room enough between their base and its bank for a fine belt of cultivated fields, which, with but few intervals, extends nearly its whole length. The portion of the Pass east of the stream is elevated some sixty or seventy feet above that which lies to the west of it, and, being much broader, strikes the eye as an upper table, stretching with a very regular and gradual ascent to the base of the wall of mountains on that side. The road from Saltillo to Agua Nueva, for the first five miles, continues along this upper plain to the point where is situated the hacienda San Juan de la Buena Vista,[A] a collection of *adobe**

[A] The engraved Plan of the Battle is referred to by letters and figures.

* *A-do-be;* large bricks made of clay and straw, and sun-dried.

buildings, with flat roofs and walls of great thickness, and capable of good defence against any troops without artillery. This little village enjoys a commanding view, not only of the whole Pass, but of the beautiful ranges of mountains which extend from Palomas and the Rinconada on toward Monclova, and also of the valley of La Encantada, with, far to the southward, the lofty peak of Catana, towering to the clouds in the blue distance.

For the next mile the road runs over a series of dry *barrancas*, or ravines, which cross it diagonally from the mountains on the left. It then descends to the lower level, where it follows a very narrow strip of land lying between the stream and several abrupt spurs of the upper table, which jut out upon it, and which are separated from each other, at unequal intervals, by barrancas much broader and deeper than the first, and parallel with them. Thence, onward, it winds gradually upward to the plain of La Encantada. At the point where the lower level is first struck in going southward, the strip of land between the first and highest spur and the perpendicular bank of the stream, is barely wide enough for the passage of the road. That point is called LA ANGOSTURA,[B] — "The Narrows." Opposite, and in advance of it, the stream has worn a series of deep channels or gullies,[C] which form a perfect net-work, extending nearly across the whole lower level to the mountains on the right, and present in themselves a formidable obstacle to the progress of any species of troops whatever; being upwards of twenty feet in depth, with sides so precipitous as to prevent their being ascended, except at two narrow places, without the assistance of scaling-ladders.* Immediately to the left of La Angostura, a long point of land,[D] which constitutes the first and highest spur, as before remarked, advances from the upper table and terminates bluff to the road, which, towards the south, it commands for a great distance. Its sides are exceedingly steep, and its other extremity unites with a broad plateau above, which continues back to the mountains. This plateau[E] is over four hundred yards in width nearest the road, and

---

* It is the opinion of Inspector-General Churchill, who examined the ground carefully, that cavalry and infantry might have crossed them, without much difficulty, at two points; viz. one midway between the stream and the mountains, and the other near their base.

some two hundred yards at its upper termination. In rear of it there is a deep ravine,[F] too precipitous for the passage of artillery, and very difficult for cavalry; in front, there is another,[G] still deeper and more difficult; thence, all the way to La Encantada, the whole Pass to the left of the stream is a succession of alternate ridges and barrancas, wonderfully calculated to cripple the movements of cavalry and artillery, and to deprive infantry of any advantage it might otherwise possess by superiority in numbers. La Angostura, the high ridge connecting it with the plateau, and the plateau itself, being, therefore, the most easy to be defended by a small army against a large one, were selected as the positions to be occupied by ours, should the necessity of abandoning Agua Nueva arise from Santa Anna's bringing against us a force greatly superior in the first two arms just named, which could there operate with freedom and rapidity, but here would be nearly paralyzed.

Between the 10th and the 20th of February, the time was diligently employed in reconnoitring the roads and approaches, and in improving our troops in drill and discipline. General Taylor placed the whole camp, and the instruction of the troops, under the command and the direction of General Wool, whose long experience, skill, and activity peculiarly fitted him for that responsible and arduous duty; and each day's improvement gave evidence of his indefatigable exertions, as well as of the aptness and intelligence of the volunteers who were taught under his superintendence.

Every day brought fresh rumors of the approach of Santa Anna with an army whose numerical strength, compared with that of ours, was sufficient to cause all to feel that the coming struggle must be of the most sanguinary character. Every man, therefore, however humble in rank, seemed to nerve himself for the contest, as if success depended on his individual efforts. The inhabitants of Saltillo, and even those of Monterey, began rapidly to desert those cities; the few who were friendly to us warning us of our imminent peril, and the many who were inimical wearing a look of insolent exultation at the prospect of our speedy destruction. Our guards, night and day, occupied every road and pass leading to our position, as well as to the city in our rear; and our patrols and spies were thrown far out into the country on every side. Still, until the 20th of February, nothing could be discovered that would serve to corroborate the reports, which we were continually receiving through the medium of the Mexicans themselves, of the advance of their army.

It was well known that General Miñon, with a brigade consisting of 2000 of the choicest cavalry of the Republic, still hovered near us; his head-quarters for the most of the time being at the hacienda of Potosí, some sixty miles in a southeasterly direction from Agua Nueva; a point, from which he could easily hold communication, both with Santa Anna and with the citizens of Saltillo and the neighboring country; with the former by large forces, if necessary, by a high road running by the way of La Encarnacion, or by that of Matahuala to the south, and with the latter by spies, who could cross over the mountains at almost any point, or pass through them by intricate defiles, of which we were entirely ignorant.

On Saturday, the 20th of February, a strong reconnoitring party, consisting of two companies of the 1st Dragoons, two companies of the 2d Dragoons, a section of Washington's Battery, 4th Artillery, under Lieutenant O'Brien, and a sufficient number of volunteer cavalry to make in all a force of 400 mounted men, — the whole commanded by Brevet Lieutenant-Colonel May, of the 2d Dragoons, — was sent to the valley in which is situated the hacienda of Potosí, with a view, not only to ascertain the presence of Miñon's brigade, but likewise to discover, if possible, whether the enemy might not be advancing in force through that valley toward Palomas Pass,* or approaching Buena Vista by the La Hedionda route.

Colonel May was ordered not to attack the enemy, but to avoid him, if possible; the purpose of his march being solely that of observation. At the same time that he was sent in this direction, Major Benjamin McCulloch, with a small party of Texan spies, was

---

* By great exertions the Mexican army might have come through this Pass, and entered the valley north of Saltillo. It is fair to say, however, that many who have examined this difficult defile are of a contrary opinion. See the Map of the country around Buena Vista.

ordered toward La Encarnacion, for a similar object.

The rancho of La Hedionda and the hacienda of Potosí are situated, respectively, on the western and eastern sides of the same valley, and are about thirty miles distant from each other. Between them there extends, without any interruption, a level plain. At three o'clock in the afternoon, Colonel May arrived at La Hedionda, and immediately sent out piquets in various directions, to take a sweeping view of the whole valley. Hardly had he done so, when signal-fires were lighted on several peaks to the right and left of his position, and a large one near the top of the towering mountain in the immediate neighborhood of Potosí, the smoke of which could be seen at a great distance. Immense clouds of dust were soon afterwards observed to rise in the direction of the hacienda, indicating evidently the march of troops. To the left of La Hedionda, there is a long range of hills shooting off into the valley, like a spur, from the chain of mountains which lies between Agua Nueva and that place, and stretching about half way across the plain. The clouds of dust appeared to be moving around the distant point of those hills from the right. Colonel May was aware that directly over this range of hills, and only five miles distant, was another rancho, called Guachuchil, and that there passed by it a road from Potosí to Agua Nueva, which came into that over which he had just marched, midway from where he then was to the latter place. He therefore imagined that the clouds of dust, which had moved around in the direction of Guachuchil, were raised by General Miñon's brigade, on its march to get a position between him and our main army, for the purpose of intercepting his return. To be sure whether such was the fact, he directed Lieutenant Sturgis, of the 2d Dragoons, with one man to accompany him, to proceed to the top of the range of hills before mentioned, in order to reconnoitre the valley in the neighborhood of the rancho beyond. This was at about five o'clock in the afternoon; and, as the ascent was very difficult, it was nearly sunset before the Lieutenant arrived at the summit. No sooner had he done so, however, than his comrades at La Hedionda heard a heavy volley of musketry at that point, and supposed he and the man with him had fallen into an ambuscade, and been sacrificed. Night setting in, and some of the piquets, which had been expected to return before dark, not having yet come back, it was feared that they, too, had met with a similar fate. These events led Colonel May to believe that the enemy's troops, in considerable force, were very near him; but where they were exactly, and in what numbers, he was wholly at a loss to determine. The *peones* at the rancho were exceedingly terrified, and either could not, or would not, impart any information on the subject. Colonel May decided to stay where he was until morning, and not to abandon the valley until he should know definitely what had been the fate of the officers and men whom he had detached. As he had no doubt he should be attacked during the night, he prepared at once for a vigorous defence of his position. Bales of cotton, which were found at the rancho in great abundance, were placed at each end of a street running through it; and, at each temporary breastwork thus formed, Lieutenant O'Brien had one of his pieces. The men were dismounted to occupy the different buildings and yards, while the horses were kept saddled and ready for any immediate service that circumstances might require.

The long hours of watching and anxiety wore slowly away, and the uncertainty, as to what had befallen the gallant fellows who were absent, filled every heart with despondency. By nine o'clock, all the piquets had returned but one, of twelve men, commanded by Lieutenant Wood, of the 2d Dragoons; but none of them had seen any thing of the enemy. As Lieutenant Wood and his party, and Lieutenant Sturgis, if alive and at liberty, should have been back hours before, there no longer remained a doubt but that they had either been destroyed or captured.

It was past ten o'clock, when a man, dressed like one of the peones at the rancho, desired to speak with Colonel May. This man * communicated the important intelligence, that General Miñon was not only within a short distance,† but that Santa Anna himself, with an army of 30,000 men, was at La Encarnacion *that* morning, and would

---

* "A deserter from the regiment of *Coraceros*, a native of Saltillo, named Francisco Valdés, passed over from La Encarnacion to the enemy, and gave him information of the movement. The execrable treason of this infamous wretch frustrated the best combinations." — *Santa Anna's Report of the Battle.*

† He was then at Guachuchil.

attack General Taylor, at Agua Nueva, the following day.

To stay at La Hedionda a moment longer was out of the question. Colonel May had all the regular cavalry of General Taylor's army, and a section of his artillery, — a number and description of troops that could not be spared in the event of an engagement; and it was instantly determined to make a forced march during the night, in order to join him before the battle should begin. The signal to advance was immediately made known to the enemy, by the discharge of two muskets on the very eminence where it was believed poor Sturgis had fallen; and two or three new fires blazed up on the adjacent mountains. Every one supposed that they were intended to give General Miñon intelligence of the moment when the column should commence its return, and that he had already arrived at the junction of the two roads, or was making a rapid march thither, to cut it off. Every thing was accordingly prepared for instant combat. A strong advance-guard was thrown far to the front, and flankers were sent out two hundred yards to the right and left, to prevent surprise. The artillery kept the road, ready to come into battery at the shortest notice, being supported on the right and left by the 1st and 2d Dragoons, respectively, while the volunteer force brought up the rear. When the column had got well into the pass through the mountains, new signals, to indicate that it had done so, were made on their summits by the burning of fire-balls. Thus it moved on in the cold and the darkness, every man believing the next moment would find him in deadly encounter with the enemy, yet determined to cut his way to the support of the devoted little army remaining with our brave old general.

Contrary to expectation, General Miñon did not make an attack, as he should have done. The night wore away, the deep defiles and narrow valleys were successively passed, and, before daybreak on the morning of the 21st of February, the column again joined the main army, after a march of sixty miles in less than twenty-one hours. The party under Lieutenant Wood also came in shortly afterwards. He had not been surprised, as all had feared, but had been unable to find the rancho in the darkness, until after Colonel May had left it;

and, what appeared remarkable, he had not discovered a single trace of the enemy in his whole tour.

So far the expedition, with the exception of the loss of Lieutenant Sturgis and the dragoon who was with him, had been exceedingly fortunate. It was now known beyond a doubt, that the Mexican army was really near us, and meditating an immediate attack. By twelve o'clock on the 21st, Major McCulloch likewise returned, and confirmed all that Colonel May had heard, except as to the prospect of Santa Anna's arriving at Agua Nueva that day. The Major had been in the immediate vicinity of La Encarnacion, and with great adroitness had managed to get such positions as to enable him, without being observed, to see the whole force, and to estimate very nearly the strength of the different arms. He believed the whole to be upwards of 20,000 men, with a large proportion of cavalry and artillery.

As every thing now depended on the issue of the expected battle, — as the glory of the American arms, our own lives, and whatever we had hitherto gained or might hope to achieve hereafter, would be involved in the disastrous consequences of a defeat, and all must be hazarded on making one bold stand, — it was determined, after mature consideration, in order that the enemy's advantages should be diminished as much as possible, to abandon Agua Nueva, and to fall back on the position in front of Buena Vista. *That* point could not well be turned; and the nature of the ground, as has already been remarked, would seriously obstruct the operations of Santa Anna's cavalry and artillery, his two favorite and most formidable arms. There was still another important object to be gained by this movement, which will hereafter be explained. Our little army, therefore, marched back and encamped again in the immediate neighborhood of the hacienda,[H] one mile and a half in the rear of La Angostura, at which place Colonel Hardin's First Regiment of Illinois Volunteers had alone been halted, with orders to occupy the high tongue of land[D] commanding the road. By falling back thus far from the spot selected for the final issue, the army had a better ground to encamp upon, and also, close at hand, an abundant supply of water. Another advantage was wisely anticipated from this disposition of our troops, who would thus not be obliged to await in their camp the attack, but would, at the proper moment, move forward to meet it, and thereby gain, aside from every other consideration, the moral effect which the mere fact of advancing to the conflict would be sure to produce, especially on troops unaccustomed to battle.

A considerable amount of stores was still remaining at Agua Nueva, and all the afternoon and evening of the 21st were diligently employed in bringing them away, Colonel Yell, with a part of his regiment of Arkansas Mounted Volunteers having been ordered to remain behind and protect them to the last moment.

Santa Anna did not leave La Encarnacion until noon on the 21st of February. He then put his troops in motion in the following order. Four battalions of light infantry, under General Ampudia, composed his advance-guard. This division was followed by a brigade of artillery of 16-pounders, with a regiment of engineers and their train; and these, by the park of the regiment of hussars. Then came his first division of heavy infantry, under General Lombardini, with five 12-pounders and their park. His second division, under General Pacheco, followed next, with eight 8-pounders and their park; after them, the divisions of his cavalry under General Juvera. Then followed the remainder of his cannon, with the general park and baggage, the rear being covered by a brigade of lancers under General Andrade. His artillery consisted of three 24-pounders, three 16-pounders, five 12-pounders, eight 8-pounders, and a 7-inch howitzer; in all, twenty guns, besides several siege pieces, not mounted, but drawn in wagons. Of cavalry he had 4338, without including the collateral force of 2000 under General Miñon; and his engineers, sappers, artillery, and infantry, amounted to upwards of 17,000 men.*

In this order of march the Mexican army proceeded from La Encarnacion; and, having passed the Plan de la Guerra, and the narrow defile known as the Pass of Piñones, a distance of twenty-five miles, halted, in the same order, in a little valley which ex-

---

* This estimate is based on the orders and a subsequent report of Santa Anna, and on the statements of Mexican officers and other prisoners, who fell into our hands.

tends from the latter place to the Pass of Carnero (near Agua Nueva), the light infantry, under General Ampudia, pushing on to that point.

Up to this moment, Santa Anna imagined that General Taylor remained entirely ignorant of his movement. He had taken the precaution to have General Miñon's 2000 cavalry hovering about our forces for nearly the whole winter; not so much to annoy us, as to blind us to the approach of his main army; shrewdly concluding that our spies and reconnoitring parties would mistake the advance of the latter for the occasional marches, from point to point, of the former, and not take alarm until he should be upon us in sufficient strength to destroy us at a blow. As he acted, therefore, under the impression that all his plans for concealment had thus far been successful, his purpose in sending General Ampudia forward during the night, was to occupy the Pass of Carnero, in case it should not be already in the possession of our troops and fortified. He supposed that if, by any possibility, General Taylor knew of his approach, he would certainly dispute the passage of that point;

but, if not, which appeared to him probable, he hoped to surprise him by daybreak the following morning in his camp at Agua Nueva.

It was long after dark when orders were given for the two companies of the 1st Dragoons, and a part of the regiment of Kentucky Mounted Volunteers, to return from the camp at Buena Vista to the assistance of Colonel Yell, in case the enemy should attempt to cut him off; and directions were sent to him, in the event of an attack, to fire the hacienda of Agua Nueva, and destroy the stores he might be unable to remove, and then to fall back on the position occupied by the army. It was nearly midnight when these troops arrived there. They had hardly formed, when Colonel Yell's advanced piquet, stationed in the Pass of Carnero, was attacked by the Mexican light division and driven in;* our men not even waiting to determine whether those who

---

* Our piquets had met with patrols from General Miñon's brigade on several previous occasions down this road toward La Encarnacion, and shots had been exchanged between them. Ampudia justified his firing, and the risk of thereby alarming our camp, by saying he believed our men had mistaken his own for General Miñon's troops.

fired upon them were mounted or on foot. The order was immediately given to set fire to the buildings, and at the same time the whole train of both loaded and empty wagons moved off with furious speed for Buena Vista; the troops remaining behind until all the stores were consumed.

The burning of the buildings, and of several large stacks of unthreshed grain, illumined the whole valley of La Encantada, and painted the rugged and picturesque features of the surrounding mountains in bright relief against the murky shadows of the intervening gorges. Perhaps no single picture of some of the most striking effects of war could produce a stronger or more lasting impression, than the one here exhibited. The noise of the falling timbers, the roar of the flames, the huge column of ascending smoke, the appearance of armed and mounted men moving between the spectator and the fire, with the brilliant light flashing here and there on burnished arms and glittering appointments, — taken in connection with the scattered shots interchanged between still other of our advanced parties and those of Ampudia, the heavy rumbling of our rapidly retreating train of wagons, intermingled with the distant trumpet-signals now and then faintly heard in the direction of the approaching enemy,—all conspired to render that cold, deep midnight, one which could never be forgotten. Besides, the scene of that conflagration, with its attendant circumstances, was invested with another and more fearful interest; for it awakened the reflection, that the coming morrow was to behold the two armies, now so near each other, in mortal strife, the issue of which no one could contemplate without intense anxiety.

It was daybreak on the morning of the 22d of February, when all our cavalry had returned to Buena Vista, leaving the whole valley of La Encantada open to the enemy. But before that time Santa Anna had again put the heavy masses of his column in motion for the Pass of Carnero,* being still under the impression that he should be able to come suddenly upon General Taylor's force at Agua Nueva, and to cut it up before it could be suitably disposed for battle. Great, therefore, was his astonishment on coming through the mountain gorge, far enough to command a view of that place, to find it entirely abandoned. At first he imagined our forces had retired

BATTLE OF BUENA VISTA. 27

under the cover of intrenchments, which he had heard we had thrown up; and he immediately directed his troops so as to turn our right, in order to gain La Encantada and the road between us and Saltillo, in accordance with a part of one of his three previous plans of operation. But, upon approaching the ruins of the hacienda, a Mexican servant, whom he found there, informed him that our army had been evacuating its position ever since the preceding day, and had fallen back toward the city. By this movement, all his purposes, based upon the expectation of resistance at Agua Nueva, were rendered abortive. But this masterly strategy of our commander, in his change of position, was then, as had been calculated, construed by Santa Anna into a precipitate retreat. Therefore, without pausing to refresh his already exhausted troops, he pushed on with his whole cavalry force and his light division, to cut us to pieces. This he believed he could the more readily accomplish, as he had previously ordered General Miñon, with his 2000 choice troops, to get in rear of us, if possible, at Buena Vista; if not, by the Pass of Palomas Adentro, and a narrow and winding pathway over the mountains to the valley east of Saltillo.* Supposing that order already executed, he indulged the hope that he could yet entrap, between two formidable portions of his army, what he imagined to be our panic-stricken and fugitive columns. Elated by such a brilliant prospect, he urged more rapidly forward his weary and nearly famished troops, leaving directions for his artillery and heavy infantry to follow as fast as possible.

Thus, by General Taylor's falling back to Buena Vista, he caused Santa Anna to become inspired with the hope just mentioned. Under its influence, he compelled his whole army, already suffering from thirst and worn down by the fatigue of a continuous march of thirty-five miles over a desert, to hurry on fourteen more, without rest, and with only the refreshment of a meagre repast and a single draught of water.

---

* General Miñon says in his Report, that Santa Anna did not direct or suggest the latter movement until the evening of the 22d; that before that time he (General Miñon) had taken the responsibility of moving thither, and had gained a position east of the town, as soon as he could do so after he had learned that General Taylor had fallen back on Buena Vista. Santa Anna himself is the opposing authority.

No calculations could have had results more fortunate than those of General Taylor. Santa Anna had cherished the vain belief that his antagonist remained totally ignorant of his movements; and, by his extreme solicitude to keep up that ignorance until the moment of attack, he permitted himself to be completely out-generalled, even on this very point. For his own place and condition were perfectly known, while he himself remained, as he unwillingly admits, entirely in the dark as to those of General Taylor, whose retrograde and apparently confused and hurried march decoyed him into what he has since termed a Thermopylæ. It is very doubtful if, with all his superiority of numbers, he could have been induced to venture to this spot, had not his elation at the prospect of our speedy destruction borne him so far forward before he was undeceived as to our flight, that he could not recede, nor avoid a battle, without disgrace.

He was, therefore, singularly unfortunate in thus having the scene of his anticipated engagement so suddenly, unexpectedly, and, as it were, mysteriously changed from a known to an unknown point. Nor was he less so as to the *time* he had selected for it. If, in the whole year, there be one day, above all others, when the heart of an American is naturally animated by the purest sentiments of patriotism, — when all that is greatest and best in his country's history is brought most vividly to his mind, as an example that should strengthen his purpose, and nerve his arm, to emulate the glorious deeds of the Past, — that is the day which gave birth to THE FATHER OF HIS COUNTRY. But it was on the morning of Washington's Birthday, that Santa Anna indulged in the delusive hope, that an army of Americans, unmindful of its sublime associations, and recreant to their country and their name, had basely fled before him.

It was eight o'clock when the "long roll" called our men to arms. No one, who there witnessed the cheerful alacrity with which they seized their weapons, and sprang to their places in the lines, — who saw the firm resolve impressed on every countenance in that determined little band, — can ever forget the sight.

Every banner was unfurled to the bright sun and enlivening breeze; and, as the various bands of music struck up the national air of

BATTLE OF BUENA VISTA. 31

"*Hail, Columbia,*" the sacred battle-cry, — "THE MEMORY OF WASHINGTON!" — passed from regiment to regiment, and from corps to corps, amid the most enthusiastic shouts.

Could the friends at home, of those here marshalled for the conflict, have seen the spirit which animated them; could they have beheld them cut off from the hope of returning with honor to all they loved, except through their own brave exertions, surrounded,* as they were, by foes bent on their destruction, proverbially merciless, smarting under the disgrace of recent defeats, and now about to fight under the immediate eye of their most distinguished general; — could their dearest friends have seen them thus, not one but would have glowed with pride at their gallant bearing, and would himself have girded on their arms, and, invoking for them the aid of the God of Battles, would, in the spirit of the heroic past, have bid them go forth to victory, or, if it must be, to the sacrifice.

---

* The 2000 cavalry, under General Miñon, had already come through the Pass of Palomas Adentro in rear of us; and General Urrea and General Romero, with another brigade of cavalry, had previously been sent through the mountains by the way of Tula, and were at this time on the road east of Monterey. — *See Santa Anna's Report.*

General Taylor had not yet returned from Saltillo, whither he had proceeded, on the evening of the 21st, with a small force, to make dispositions for its defence. General Wool, therefore, being next to him in rank, commanded the troops during his absence, and now gave the order to move forward to the battle-ground. It was received with three hearty cheers, when the regiments and corps broke into column, and each, to the time of some lively air, moved rapidly off to its position.

In the mean time, Santa Anna's cavalry came thundering along the valley of La Encantada, and down the road through the Pass, a vast cloud of dust distinctly marking its progress. The first evidence it received, that any check would be offered to its onward course to Saltillo, was the sight of Washington's Battery of eight pieces, which had been directed by General Wool to occupy La Angostura, and was then advancing over the crest of a ridge, and descending the slope of the road leading to that position; and of the First Regiment of Illinois Volunteers, which was already on the high ridge to the left of it. As soon as the enemy discovered this force, and before he had come within range of Washington's guns, his bugles sounded a halt. Immediately afterwards, all the more advanced squadrons wheeled about, and retired behind a protecting elevation of the ground,[1] while those in the rear came rapidly up, and formed upon them. In a short time, their compact and serried masses, thus accumulated, with their flags and pennons flying, and their bright lances sparkling in the sun, extended from the stream nearly half way to the mountains on our left.

By this time General Wool had placed our troops in their several positions,* and the following was the order of battle for the 22d of February. Captain Washington's Battery occupied the road at La Angostura, supported by Colonel Hardin's First Regiment of Illinois Volunteers, posted, as before remarked, on the elevated tongue of land which extends from that point to the plateau. The Second Regiment of Illinois Volunteers and one company of Texans, the whole under Colonel Bissell, were on its left, and

---

* That is, the *very first* positions of the several regiments and corps. Every change they afterwards made is noted in the text.

near the foot of the plateau; while the Second Regiment of Kentucky Volunteers, under Colonel McKee, occupied the crest of a ridge in the rear of Washington's Battery, around which the road, divided, runs. The Arkansas and Kentucky Regiments of Mounted Volunteers, commanded, severally, by Colonel Yell and Colonel Marshall, were stationed on the extreme left, near the base of the mountains; while the brigade of Indiana Volunteers, under General Lane (composed of the Second Regiment, commanded by Colonel Bowles, and the Third by Colonel Lane), the First Regiment of Mississippi Riflemen under Colonel Jefferson Davis, Captain Steen's squadron of the 1st Dragoons, Lieutenant-Colonel May's squadron of the 2d Dragoons, and the light Batteries of Captains Sherman and Bragg, occupied, as a reserve, the next ridges immediately in rear of the right of the plateau and of the ground of the Illinois Volunteers. In this position our army awaited the attack.

The situation of the troops was now such that most of them could command a view of the upper end of the pass and the opening to the valley beyond. The enemy was evidently waiting for the arrival of his rear columns. In the mean time, General Taylor had returned from Saltillo. As he rode along our lines, he was everywhere received with the most enthusiastic cheers; and the sound of each wild hurrah could be distinctly heard by those of the Mexican army who had already arrived on their ground.

General Wool also rode along the lines, and addressed a few spirited and patriotic remarks to each regiment and corps which he passed. He reminded the troops of his own column particularly of their past labors, and their protracted and weary marches[*] to find the enemy, who now stood before them in sufficient strength to give them all they could require in the way of combat, and to afford *every* man an opportunity to win all the distinction he could wish. And he suggested to the minds of all the great good fortune which was theirs, to be called more signally to mark the anniversary of a day already hallowed to their country, and one on which no man could be unfaithful to the trust she had confided to him, — that of maintaining the glory of her arms and the

---

[*] See Appendix, A.

lustre of the American name as bright and unsullied as they had been left by her greatest general, to whom this day had given birth. This was, likewise, responded to by three hearty cheers.

For a long time, the engineers and topographical engineers of both armies were busily employed; ours, in moving far to the front, to get a more accurate view of their different forces as they came up, and to learn their several positions, — and theirs, in gaining elevated points between the two lines, to reconnoitre our ground and the disposition of our troops. Our exact strength they already knew from their spies and from their friends in Saltillo.

Meanwhile Santa Anna sent in a flag of truce* to General Taylor, with the following note:

"HEAD-QUARTERS OF THE LIBERATING
ARMY OF THE REPUBLIC.

"You are surrounded by twenty thousand men, and cannot, in any human probability, avoid suffering a rout

---

* The bearer of this flag was a German named Vanderlinden, then the Surgeon-General of the Mexican army. He seemed very anxious to impress upon the mind of the officer who met him the important fact, that Santa Anna had *twenty-three generals* with him.

and being cut to pieces with your troops. But, as you deserve from me consideration and particular esteem, I wish to save you from a catastrophe; and for that purpose I give you this notice, in order that you may surrender at discretion, under the assurance that you will be treated with the consideration belonging to the Mexican character. To this end, you will be granted an hour's time to make up your mind, to commence from the moment when a flag of truce arrives in your camp. With this view, I assure you of my particular consideration.

"God and Liberty! Camp at Encantada, February 22, 1847.
"ANTO. LOPEZ DE SANTA ANNA.
"To GENERAL Z. TAYLOR,
"*Commanding the Forces of the United States.*" *

In answer to the foregoing, General Taylor immediately despatched this note:

"HEAD-QUARTERS, ARMY OF OCCUPATION,
Near Buena Vista, Feb. 22, 1847.

"Sir: In reply to your note of this date, summoning me to surrender my forces at discretion, I beg leave to say that I decline acceding to your request.

"With high respect, I am, Sir, your obedient servant,
"Z. TAYLOR,
"*Major-General U. S. A., Commanding.*
"Señor General D. ANTO. LOPEZ DE SANTA ANNA,
"*Commanding in chief, Encantada.*"

---

* See Appendix, C.

A short time afterwards,* the whole of the Mexican army had come up and been formed upon their ground in the following order:

The first and second divisions of infantry were placed in two lines, one in rear of the other, on one of the ridges in front of our position; there being another and rather more elevated one between us. A battery of 16-pounders, supported by the regiment of engineers, was established on a higher point on their right; and two others, of 12 and 8 pounders, and the 7-inch howitzer, on their left and near the road. The latter were placed in battery by Santa Anna in person; the former, by his Chief of Engineers, General Mora y Villamil, and his Chief of Artillery, General Corona. The cavalry was then disposed in rear of his right and left flanks, and the regiment of hussars, — Santa Anna's personal guard, — in rear of the centre. There was a small eminence on his left, directly upon the road, and in front of Washington's Battery, which the beautiful battalion of Leon

---

* "We took a position and awaited the infantry, which arrived at one o'clock, having taken on the road five wagons, and some provisions and forage left by the enemy." — *Mexican Engineer's Report of the Battle.*

was ordered to occupy. The general park was placed in rear of all, and covered by the brigade of General Andrade. Santa Anna's own position was the same as that of his hussars.

It was past two o'clock before all these arrangements had been completed. In the interval, General Ampudia and Colonel Baneneli, with the four battalions of light infantry, were directed to get possession of one of two gradual slopes [J] of the mountain to the left of the plateau. This movement being observed, a portion of the Arkansas and Kentucky Volunteers, and a small battalion from the Indiana brigade, all on foot, and armed with rifles, were placed under the command of Colonel Marshall, and sent up the other slope [K] to resist them. While these troops were approaching each other, and severally climbing up their opposite ridges (which, it should be remarked, draw closer and closer together, and finally unite near the summit of the mountain), each evidently endeavoring to outflank the other, a movement was made on the enemy's left, which induced General Taylor to order a corresponding one on our right. Accordingly, Captain Bragg's Light

Battery, with Colonel McKee's Regiment of Kentucky foot Volunteers as a support, was sent across the stream, to occupy a position between it and the mountains on that side, and somewhat in advance of the Battery at La Angostura.

Captain Washington had already detached two of his pieces, which were sent up to the left of the plateau, under Lieutenant Bryan, of the Topographical Engineers, then temporarily on duty in the artillery, — when he was asked by General Wool, if he could spare still another.

"Yes," said he.

"But what will become of this key to our position, if you are deprived of three of your guns?"

"I WILL DEFEND IT," was his gallant reply; and he immediately detached Lieutenant O'Brien, then commanding his first section, with another piece.

When this gun was joined to the section already on the plateau, Lieutenant O'Brien took command of the whole; the Second Regiment of Indiana Volunteers being ordered up to sustain him.

At three o'clock precisely, the enemy opened

the battle by firing a shell from his howitzer at this part of our lines. Immediately afterwards, Ampudia's light division became warmly engaged with our riflemen, on the side of the mountain; the former discharging their pieces in continuous and rapid volleys; the latter, lying behind the crest of their ridge, firing deliberately, and doing terrible execution with their unerring weapons. From that time until dark, these troops continued the conflict without changing their positions, except to approach each other by climbing still higher up the mountain, until, at last, there were two lines of combatants from near the plateau to its very summit.

The fighting in this quarter, together with an occasional cannonade, directed by the enemy at the troops on the plateau, constituted the action of the 22d; the two armies not becoming regularly engaged on that day. At dark, a shell was thrown into the air by the enemy, as a signal for his light division to cease the contest; and not a gun was fired afterwards, by either side, for the whole night, except a few shots now and then exchanged between the advanced piquets and moving patrols of the two forces.

The loss on the American side during this day's contest was very trifling, four men only being wounded; while that of the Mexican army was over three hundred,* in killed and wounded.

By night fall, Colonel Hardin's First Regiment of Illinois Volunteers had completed a parapet on the high ridge it occupied, extending along its whole front; and, under the direction of our engineers, had dug a ditch and thrown up an epaulment in front of Washington's Battery, with a traverse upon its right, continuing the ditch and a slight breastwork from thence to the brink of the impassable gullies of the stream. This ditch was occupied by an immediate supporting force de-

---

* "The enemy, so soon as he perceived that we had occupied the height that flanked his left and our right, detached two battalions to dislodge us, which led to a warm engagement, that lasted all the afternoon and till after dark, when he was repulsed with a loss of four hundred men, according to the report of the prisoners. Ours was much less, as we had the advantage of the ground." — *Santa Anna's Report of the Battle.*

"The enemy tried in vain to dislodge them [Ampudia's light battalions] from their position, by moving against it a heavy column; and was compelled to retire, leaving the ravine [between the two slopes] filled with wounded." — *Mexican Engineer's Report.*

tached from Colonel Hardin's regiment, consisting of two companies, and commanded by Lieutenant-Colonel Weatherford. To provide for the contingency of the advance of our batteries during the battle, a small opening was left between the left of the epaulment and the high bluff, sufficiently wide for the passage of cannon. But, in order to prevent the enemy from having the advantage of it in case of an assault, it was choked up by two wagons, laden with stones, and having their wheels locked by chains. They could easily be removed by us, and the way be opened in case of necessity.

Early in the day, General Miñon, with his brigade, had entered the valley east of Saltillo, as Santa Anna had anticipated; but the latter, finding General Taylor had made a stand and was determined to offer him battle, sent directions to the former to remain in that quarter, and to fall upon us during our retreat before his overwhelming masses. In order the more certainly to insure that none of our army should escape, a thousand mounted rancheros, armed with lances and *machetes*,*

---

* *Ma-che-te*, a kind of long, heavy knife, similar to those used in cutting down Indian corn.

who had been collected at Monclova, Buenaventura, and Parras, and were commanded by Colonel Miguel Blanco and Colonel Aguierra, were also sent from Patos, by a mule-path leading through the mountains, into the same valley. While, therefore, General Miñon was to hover about the east side of the road leading from Saltillo to Monterey, along which, it was supposed, we should soon be flying in great confusion, Colonels Blanco and Aguierra were to occupy the small town of Capellania on the west, likewise to await our retreat, and to assist in cutting us up without quarter.

General Taylor, feeling convinced from the dispositions of Santa Anna, that he would defer making his grand attack until the next morning, and fearing that the strong force in the rear of the city, where all our stores were, might make a movement to take it, left General Wool in command, and again, at sunset, started from the field, with Colonel May's squadron of the 2d Dragoons, and Colonel Davis's Regiment of Mississippi Riflemen, for Saltillo, the better to provide for such an emergency. On arriving there, he arranged that Warren's and Webster's commands should remain to garrison the town and redoubt, respectively, as they had previously done; and that the train and head-quarters camp, then established on the brow of the hill immediately south of the town, should be defended by one 6-pounder, detached from Captain Bragg's Battery, and under the command of Lieutenant Shover, with a support of two companies of Colonel Davis's riflemen, under Captain Rogers.

After the action of the 22d had drawn to a close, Santa Anna made a final address to those of his troops that remained in our front. He referred to the wrongs which, he said, had been inflicted upon their country by the barbarians of the North; wrongs which could not be submitted to without eternal disgrace, and which could be redressed only by the last resort of nations. The United States of the North had, coward-like, presumed on their strength alone, and wantonly set at defiance every principle of right. They had provoked this war under the cover of other objects to be gained, but really for their own aggrandizement, and the acquisition of territory clearly the property of the United States of the South. The one country aimed only at the entire destruction of the nationality of the other. He wished to call their whole attention to that single fact; and not only to that, but to a thousand others, which, like that, would make them burn to take terrible vengeance on the mercenary invaders of their soil. He called upon them to look upon their country. What met their sight? Its possessions wrested away; its dignity insulted; its fair fields ravaged; its citizens slaughtered; its hearths and homes made desolate. Others had gone forth to vindicate these wrongs, but they had fallen; and now their blood, which had drenched the fields of Palo Alto, Resaca de la Palma, and Monterey, called on them, their brethren, with an eloquence that must reach their hearts, to avenge their death. He reminded them, that they had crossed deserts, had suffered hunger, and thirst, and fatigue, without a murmur. Long and weary had been their march; but now they should be rewarded with repose, and the enjoyment of the abundance which filled the ample granaries of the murderers of their brethren. He concluded by saying, that we were but a handful, and at his mercy; that he had magnanimously offered to spare our lives, and even to treat us with consideration; but that we had vain-gloriously rejected his clemency, leaving, as the only alternative, our utter extermination, without pity or quarter.*

This address was received with loud cries of "*Viva Santana!*" "*Viva la Republica!*" "*Libertad o Muerte!*"—distinctly heard in our lines. After the shouting had ceased, Santa Anna's own magnificent band commenced playing; and, as the gentle breeze swept down the Pass toward us, each delicious strain seemed to float upon it, mellowed by distance, yet distinct and inexpressibly sweet. For over half an hour it continued to delight our "barbarian ears" with the exquisitely beautiful airs of the sunny south. When it had finished, and the last faint echo had sunk to rest, silence the most profound fell over the two armies like a pall. The huge mountains on each side reared their craggy heads high into the darkness above, and the Pass itself seemed to lie between them in deep gloom and utter solitude. No one could realize that there were so many thousands of human beings gathered together in that narrow gorge. And it was a dreadful reflection,

---

* The substance of this address was repeated to some of our officers by Mexicans who heard it.

that so many of them, now full of life, and ambition, and high aspirations; now visiting in thought their far-off homes and the dear ones there; now the objects of pride and yearning solicitude; now the centre of deep affection, of sacred love, and of long-cherished hopes, — would be stricken down in the full flush and vigor of manhood, and, ere another night should cast its dark mantle over the earth, would be numbered for ever among the things that were.

At ten o'clock in the evening, the two companies of the 1st Dragoons were ordered by General Wool to return to Buena Vista, strike our camp, pack it in wagons, and then to park these carefully in one of the hollows between the hacienda and La Angostura. This service was completed by half past one o'clock, and the whole train arranged so as to be moved at the shortest notice.

Until eleven o'clock on the evening of the 22d, the weather was quite mild; but at that hour a cold wind began to blow, and the sky, which before had been thickly overcast, became filled with dark and heavy drifts of clouds, which now and then let down slight showers of rain, more particularly up the mountain on our left. There the men suffered extremely from the cold. They gathered together the trunks of the *yuca* and the dry stalks of the *sotol*, and built themselves fires, until at length, up the whole side of the mountain, from near the plateau to the very top, light after light was kindled; and for the whole night long each one was surrounded by a circle of shivering troops. All the rest of both armies remained in position, and slept upon their arms without fires.*

About two o'clock in the morning of the 23d, some of our advanced piquets were attacked by those of the Mexican army, and driven in; and, between that time and daybreak, the light division of General Ampudia was reënforced by 2000 infantry from the divisions of Generals Lombardini and Pacheco. Many of Ampudia's command, when it had thus been augmented, clambered along near the summit of the mountain, and succeeded in gaining elevated positions to the left and

---

* "In our position we passed the night, which was absolutely infernal, owing to the cold, rain, and wind, which last almost amounted to a hurricane, while we had neither food nor fuel." —*Mexican Engineer's Report.*

50   BATTLE OF BUENA VISTA.

rear of our riflemen. It was also in this quarter, at the very first dawn of day, that the battle of the 23d commenced.

General Wool, perceiving that the strength of the enemy in that direction was much greater than on the evening before, immediately detached Major Trail, of the 2d Illinois Volunteers, with another small battalion of riflemen, including Captain Conner's company of Texas Volunteers, to reënforce the command which had there engaged the enemy with much spirit, and, although contending with nearly eight to one, continued to maintain very handsomely its own part of the mountain. It was soon assisted, likewise, by Lieutenant O'Brien, who, with the 2d Indiana Volunteers, had remained at the upper edge [L] of the plateau for the night. His pieces were one 12-pounder howitzer, one 6-pounder gun, and one 4-pounder. Just at sunrise, as great numbers of Ampudia's light troops poured down into the ravine which divided their slope of the mountain from the one occupied by our riflemen, he pushed forward his howitzer, and, although the distance and elevation were very great, succeeded in throwing directly into the midst of them some six or eight spherical-

BATTLE OF BUENA VISTA. 51

case shot, which, exploding just at the proper time, did immense execution. Up to this moment the discharge of the enemy's musketry on the side of the mountain had been incessant; but, at the bursting of the first shot, it completely ceased for several minutes, his troops being occupied in climbing still higher up and out of range. The accuracy and effect of Lieutenant O'Brien's firing on this occasion were so admirable, as to call forth the cheers of our whole line.

In the mean time, the chief of Santa Anna's staff, General Micheltorena, succeeded in planting a battery of 8-pounders at the upper termination of the elevated ridge ^(M) already spoken of as lying between our position and that of the enemy, from which point he had a plunging fire on the plateau. His first efforts were against the pieces under Lieutenant O'Brien, but the distance was so great, that the latter did not attempt to answer him.

While the battle was thus opened and continued by the small force on our extreme left, the rest of our troops, under the direction of General Wool, were placed in their final position to await the attack then menaced in our front. Captain Bragg's Battery, supported by

Colonel McKee's regiment, remained at the same point [N] on our extreme right, to which it had been directed to proceed the evening before. Captain Washington's Battery continued to occupy La Angostura,[B] sustained by Colonel Hardin's regiment* in the trenches on its right, and upon the high spur on its left.

It should have been remarked, that the plateau is scalloped, on its side next the road, by three deep gorges, that run back into it. They are of unequal length; the shortest[O] being only a little in advance of the point where the high tongue of land, occupied by the 1st Illinois Volunteers, joins the upper plain; the next[P] still longer; and the third[Q] running back more than half way from the road to the mountain. The six companies† of Colonel Bissell's Second Regiment of Illinois Volunteers, which remained, were posted on the plateau opposite to the head of the middle gorge.[R]

---

* That is, eight companies of it; Captain Morgan's and Captain Prentiss's companies composing a part of Major Warren's command in Saltillo.

† Two were in Saltillo, Captain Hacker's and Captain Wheeler's, — and two (besides the Texan company), Captain Lemon's and Captain Woodward's, composed the battalion sent to the mountain under Major Trail.

BATTLE OF BUENA VISTA. 53

On their left, and a little retired, was one 12-pounder howitzer, under Lieutenant French, and on their right, and also a little in the rear, one 6-pounder gun, under Lieutenant Thomas. Both these pieces belonged to Captain Sherman's Battery, the other two, under the Captain himself and Lieutenant John F. Reynolds, remaining in reserve, as on the 22d.[S] To the right and rear of Lieutenant Thomas's gun, were the two companies of the 1st Dragoons,[T] and to the right and rear of them, and near the head of the first gorge, Major McCulloch's company of Mounted Texans.[U] Colonel Bowles's Second Regiment of Indiana Volunteers occupied the extreme left of the plateau, with Lieutenant O'Brien's three pieces on their right; there being a long interval between his guns and Lieutenant French's howitzer on the left of the regiment under Colonel Bissell. Colonel Lane's Third Regiment of Indiana Volunteers occupied the small eminence[V] in rear of Washington's Battery, while all of the Arkansas and Kentucky Mounted Volunteers, who had not been detached to fight on foot, remained in the head of the broad ravine[W] in rear of the left of the plateau.

The Mexican army was formed in three

columns of attack. The first,[X] destined to move down the road and carry the Pass of La Angostura, was composed of the Regiment of Engineers, the Twelfth Regiment, the Regiment styled "*Fijo de Mexico*," the Battalion of Puebla, and the celebrated "*Guarda Costa de Tampico*." This column was commanded by General Mora y Villamil. The second column was composed of the divisions of Generals Lombardini and Pacheco, and was destined, one division[Y] to move directly across the ridge to the left of their 8-pounder battery, and the other[Z] to advance up the principal ravine in front of the plateau, where both, uniting near the mountain, were to turn the left of our force upon the plateau. The troops under General Ampudia were to compose the third,[J] destined to sweep the mountain, to turn our extreme left, and then, in conjunction with the second, to fall on our rear. The first two columns had each a strong supporting force of cavalry; moreover, the 12-pounder battery and the howitzer were brought farther forward, and established within range of La Angostura, on a slight eminence,[1] close to the road, and just to the right and rear of the small hill occupied by the battalion of

Leon.[20] This battery was to assist the attack to be made by the first column. A powerful reserve,[2] commanded by General Ortega, remained on the ground occupied, on the night of the 22d, by Santa Anna's two front lines of battle.

These arrangements, on both sides, completed the preliminaries of the grand conflict. While they were in progress, our riflemen and Ampudia's force continued hotly engaged, and the enemy's battery of 8-pounders kept up a steady fire upon our troops on the left of the plateau.[L]

As General Pacheco's division had fewer difficulties to overcome than that of General Lombardini, it had moved up the ravine and gained its position before the latter had united with it. General Lombardini's division, however, had by that time passed the summit of the height where the 8-pounder battery was posted,[M] and began to descend the declivity toward the same ravine, but at a point higher up than that already occupied by General Pacheco. Both of these divisions, as has been already remarked, were supported by large bodies of dragoons and lancers; and, while Pacheco's, being in the deep ravine in front, was concealed from view, Lombardini's was in full sight of nearly the whole of our army. And a most beautiful sight it was. The men were all in full dress, the horses were gayly caparisoned, and the arms of both cavalry and infantry shone bright as silver. Every regiment, corps, and squadron had its standards, colors, and guidons unfurled; and, while the infantry marched steadily onward with a most perfectly marked and cadenced step, the cavalry moved with the regularity and precision it would have observed in an ordinary field review.

Our lines, meanwhile, were standing quietly in position. Not a word was spoken, excepting now and then, when some subdued expression of admiration at the magnificent appearance of the enemy and the coolness with which they came forward to the combat, would involuntarily escape the lips of our brave and determined men.

It was a time never to be forgotten, that short period which intervened between the final dispositions and the moment of attack. The morning was unusually bright and clear; the sunlight seemed to cover with flashing diamonds the burnished weapons and appointments of the Mexicans; while a cool and invigorating breeze displayed every flag, and sported with the gaudy and fluttering pennons of what appeared to be a countless forest of lances. The sharp rattle of musketry, the sullen reply of the deadly rifle, and the bugle-calls, intermingled with the shouts of those who were desperately struggling high up the mountain, came down upon the ear with an eloquent distinctness. All these circumstances, taken in connection with the roar of their cannon, and the rushing sound of the balls as they tore up the ground in the midst of us, or went screaming through the air above us, will come vividly back to the memory, until they shall be old men, who, for the first time, were standing silently there to await the rude shock of battle.

Major Mansfield, of the Engineers, having reconnoitred the movements of the enemy from an advanced point, and ascertained the presence and exact position of General Pacheco's division, came back with the intelligence; when Inspector-General Churchill rode to the left of the plateau,[L] and informed General Lane, that the enemy was then coming up, and across the main ravine in front. General Lane, at this moment, was the ranking officer on the plateau; as General Wool, after superintending in person the posting of all the troops and the final arrangements for battle, had a few minutes before gone down to La Angostura, to see that every thing was in readiness for repelling the first column under General Mora y Villamil, then on the march to attack that point. General Lane, therefore, immediately ordered forward Lieutenant O'Brien, with his three pieces of artillery, and the Second Regiment of Indiana Volunteers to support him. This force advanced over two hundred yards in front of all the other troops, and, having turned the head of the third gorge, was halted; when Lieutenant O'Brien placed his section in battery, and, immediately afterwards, the column of companies displayed into line on his left, the front being changed diagonally forward towards the road.[3]

General Pacheco's infantry had, by this time, begun to ascend from the ravine, and were forming in successive lines across the narrow ridge which divides it from the gorge;[Q] his lancers still remaining behind, under cover.* General Lane's infantry had

---

* This is the time (nine o'clock, A. M.) selected to represent on the annexed Plan of the Battle the position of our

hardly completed its line, before it was opened upon by the Mexicans, then distant about two hundred yards. They were answered with promptness and great effect; and Lieutenant O'Brien's guns, which were admirably served, swept down whole platoons of them at a discharge. The disparity between the two forces then engaged was at least ten to one in favor of the enemy; and General Lane, in addition to the fire of the troops in his front, was nearly enfiladed by the 8-pounder battery on his left, which had now got so completely the range, that almost every shot took effect in his ranks. Notwithstanding this, he continued the unequal conflict for twenty-five minutes. During that time, the front lines of General Pacheco's division were repeatedly thrown into confusion; the whole of the new corps of Guanajuato, which formed its advance,

---

own and the enemy's troops; as it is considered to have been the moment when the grand conflict commenced. Colonel Davis's Mississippi Riflemen, Colonel May's Squadron of 2d Dragoons, Captain Albert Pike's Squadron of Arkansas Mounted Volunteers, and a piece of artillery under Lieutenant Kilburn, being on the march from Saltillo, were not at this exact time near enough to the field of battle to be included within the space covered by the Plan.

being either killed or dispersed. But, by his successive formations, he was enabled rapidly to supply the places of those destroyed, and to present a continuous sheet of fire. General Lane now determined to get out of the range of the battery on his left, by pushing still farther down the ridge; hoping, at the same time, to force General Pacheco back into the ravine. He, accordingly, directed Lieutenant O'Brien to limber up, and advance some fifty or sixty yards farther to the right and front; which being promptly done, the pieces were again placed in battery and commenced the slaughter.

At this time, General Lane, being himself on the left of the 2d Indiana Volunteers, which were also to move forward and sustain Lieutenant O'Brien, had the mortification to see the companies breaking off, one by one, from the right, and retreating in great confusion; Colonel Bowles, who commanded the regiment, having given, without his authority or knowledge, the order, "*Cease firing, and retreat!*" Nothing could have been more unfortunate. For, if General Lane's purpose had been promptly responded to by this regiment, which up to that moment had behaved with great gallantry, it is more than probable that General Pacheco's division would have been cut up in time to allow us to engage with our other and fresh troops that of General Lombardini, before he could have crossed the ravine above and gained the plateau. If, instead of retreating, these troops had pressed vigorously forward, the success of the day would have been more complete; and there cannot be a doubt but that hundreds of valuable lives would have been spared, which were afterwards sacrificed to regain the many and great advantages we lost in consequence of this, to say the least, ill-timed order.* Had it not been given, the patriotic state of Indiana, by a single effort of one of her regiments, would have been covered with glory.†

---

* It is but justice to state, that, among officers of long experience, the belief is entertained, that the prime fault was one of rashness, and want of judgment, in placing this force in a position, which, they contend, neither this nor any other regiment could have maintained, — a position, moreover, which, they assert, it was not necessary to hold as one upon which others depended; and that General Lane should be made to bear a part of the odium which the regiment could not escape. Other officers of equal experience express the contrary opinion, as set forth in the text.

† "About 3000 infantry, and a supporting force of caval-

General Lane and his staff endeavored, by every possible inducement, to rally the men again, but all without avail. They precipitately fled, leaving the intrepid O'Brien, and his gallant subordinate, Lieutenant Bryan, entirely without support. For some minutes they held on to their position, single-handed; their pieces, charged with two canisters at a time, sending scores on scores of the enemy into eternity. The Mexicans, however, maintained their ground with great spirit, and soon cut up Lieutenant O'Brien's men and horses to such a degree, that, when he was finally pressed upon by the whole of the immense force arrayed against him, he was compelled reluctantly to limber up two of his guns, and retire from the point he had so nobly defended. He was obliged to leave the other piece, — the 4-pounder, — in the

---

ry, commanded by General Pacheco, moved up to take this height, and at nine a heavy fire was opened. The cavalry charged at the same moment. [*Not the fact.*] Many of our corps acted badly, but much havoc, nevertheless, was made among the enemy, and the heights were carried by force of arms. We lost many men, and the new corps of Guanajuato was dispersed. IF, AT THAT JUNCTURE, WE HAD BEEN ATTACKED WITH VIGOR, WE SHOULD PROBABLY HAVE BEEN DEFEATED." — *Mexican Engineer's Report.*

hands of the enemy; not, however, until every man and horse belonging to it had been either killed or disabled.

General Pacheco immediately followed up the advantage he had purchased at so much cost; his cavalry advanced from its cover, and pressed forward on the right of his infantry; while General Lombardini succeeded, at the same time, in crossing the ravine and uniting with him. The centre column was then entire, and so formidable in numbers as to appear completely irresistible.

The 2d Illinois Volunteers, under Colonel Bissell,[R] — the squadron of 1st Dragoons, under Captain Steen,[T] — and the pieces of Lieutenants Thomas and French, — had retained their position, and received a desultory fire from a part of General Pacheco's infantry, which, during the conflict with General Lane, had succeeded in getting shelter in the third gorge. These troops were ordered to advance to a closer point just before the Indiana regiment gave way. Soon after they had gained it, and had come handsomely into action, the enemy's centre column was complete, and, being relieved from the resistance of General Lane's force, now concentrated its whole fire upon them. It was returned with deliberation and great effect. Every discharge of Thomas's and French's pieces caused their immense masses to reel and waver, as the balls, opening a wide and bloody path, went tearing through them; while the rapid musketry of the gallant troops of Illinois poured a storm of lead into their serried ranks, which literally strewed the ground with the dead and dying.

It being impossible for our handful of regular cavalry, then on the field, to gain any decided advantage by charging into such an overwhelming force, where, in one moment, it would have been completely destroyed, Captain Steen was soon directed to remove it from its perilous situation back nearly to the ravine in rear. The dragoons had hardly fallen back, and McCulloch's mounted Texans [U] taken cover in the head of the first gorge, before the enemy, having continued to advance notwithstanding his severe losses, had passed with a large portion of his troops between the left of the Illinoians and the mountain; [4] so that that regiment, — or rather the six companies of it, — and the two pieces from Sherman's battery, were soon receiving a fire in front, on their left flank, and from their left and rear, at the same moment.

Inspector-General Churchill, who remained with Colonel Bissell, seemed at this time to be one of the chosen marks for the Mexican sharp-shooters; his horse being struck by three bullets in succession, and his reins cut in two by a fourth. The Illinois troops had ever been the particular favorites of that gallant veteran; and he determined to stand by them personally, and see whether his predilections were not based upon good grounds. His pride in them was fully gratified at beholding the unflinching firmness with which they maintained their position against such an immense host. At length, perceiving the danger they were in of being completely surrounded, he ordered Colonel Bissell to fall back to a point near the ravine, to prevent that issue. As regularly as if on drill, Colonel Bissell, having directed the signal, " Cease firing," to be made, gave the command, "*Face to the rear! Battalion, about* FACE! *Battalion, forward,* MARCH!" which was executed until the danger of being outflanked was past, when again, at the command to halt, given by Inspector-General Churchill, who had walked his horse slowly in front of the retiring regiment, these cool and determined men stopped, faced about, and resumed the fire with a promptness and precision which would have done credit to any troops in the service; and all under a murderous storm of bullets from the enemy. Simple justice to these brave fellows renders it necessary that all the details of their conduct on this occasion should be given. Besides, it is an evidence of the manner in which troops, in their first battle, *can* behave, when they have been properly instructed and carefully disciplined. It is a sufficient encomium on them to say, that they had never before been under fire, and that during the short time they had been engaged (twenty minutes), they had lost, in killed and wounded, no less than eighty, including officers and men. Lieutenants Thomas and French, — the latter wounded, — had likewise been obliged to fall back; but they soon came into battery again, and, in conjunction with Colonel Bissell's regiment, commenced a well-directed fire at the enemy's left flank, as he endeavored to cross the plateau and gain our rear.

Again, in justice to those who thus manfully disputed the ground, inch by inch, against such odds, it is necessary, yet mortifying, to state, that four companies of the Arkansas Volunteers,⁽⁵⁾ which had been dismounted and ordered to the plateau a few minutes before the action began, retired almost at the first fire, and became so much dispersed, that, as companies, they were not heard of again during the battle. But a few spirited individuals of the number joined their own and other regiments, and, for the whole day, nobly discharged their duty.*

At this moment, the thunder of the battery below, at La Angostura, gave evidence that the first column of the enemy, under General Mora y Villamil, had got within its range. The rapidity of the firing, and the roar of the cannon, which caused the old mountains to groan

---

* It is contended that these troops gave way in consequence of the falling back amongst them of Colonel Bowles's regiment.* That, as individuals, they were as brave as any men in the world, cannot be doubted; but their being entirely without discipline, or any habit of strict military obedience, and their consequent want of confidence in their leaders and in each other, may be fairly assigned as the principal reasons for their precipitate retreat.

* In this supposition, an officer of high rank in the regular army, who witnessed the whole of the operations, does not concur; because, he says, the Indiana regiment did not, in its flight, pass near these four companies of Arkansas Volunteers.

and quake with the repeated echoes, convinced our whole army that the gallant Washington was making good his promise to defend that point; and many and heart-felt were the wild hurrahs that rent the air in exultation at his efforts. Nothing could withstand the terrible tempest of iron which he hurled into the compact column before him. The first shock impeded its advance; it then wavered a moment, — halted, — and finally turned in confusion, and rushed into the mouth of the third gorge,[Q] and up the great ravine in front,[G] to seek protection behind the spurs which projected upon the road.

In this splendid demonstration of the capacity of artillery, and its importance as an arm, Captain Washington completely repulsed over 4000 of the flower of the Mexican army, and convinced them, beyond a doubt, of their inability to force him from his position. He was ably supported by his remaining three subalterns, Lieutenants Brent, Whiting, and Couch, who managed the pieces with great skill, and exhibited superior courage and address throughout the whole affair.

Just as Captain Washington opened his fire, Captain Sherman, with his other section,[8] was ordered up to the plateau. He immediately came into battery near the head of the first gorge,^(o) and opened his fire; Lieutenant Reynolds of his company directing one of the pieces, and the Captain himself the other. He was in a short time supported by Colonel McKee's 2d Kentucky Volunteers, which, according to instructions given to Major Mansfield, had been sent for, to come from its position across the stream, and which was brought into action with much spirit on his right. In a few minutes more, Captain Bragg, with two of his pieces, also came up, and, passing to the left of the 1st Dragoons, wheeled into battery, having three of Captain Sherman's guns on his right, — Lieutenant Thomas's being the first, — and the fourth (Lieutenant French's) at some distance to his left. A complete line of artillery was thus formed, extending from near the head of the first gorge to the brink of the ravine in rear of the plateau, and was supported by the 1st Dragoons, the Second Regiment of Kentucky Volunteers, the six companies of Colonel Bissell's regiment, and four companies of the First Regiment of Illinois Volunteers, under their gallant Colonel Hardin, who came upon the plateau the moment General Mora y Villamil's column had been repulsed. The direction of the fire of this whole force was now toward the mountain on our left. The enemy's second column had by this time succeeded in advancing across the whole plateau; and, being within good range, every discharge of our artillery took effect upon it. The firing on our side was now incessant and most terrible; the storm of iron and lead beating against the dark masses of the Mexicans with dreadful fury. They, however, stood firm to their work, and for a while returned the fire with such determined valor, as to elicit the admiration of all who were opposed to them.

Meanwhile, their cavalry swept by between their infantry and the mountain at the head of the plateau, in rapid pursuit of the Indiana regiment; the left of General Ampudia's force leaving the foot of the slope on which they had been contending, and pressing forward with them. Those of the Arkansas and Kentucky Mounted Volunteers, who had remained near the head of the ravine, were obliged immediately to give way before this force, which came pouring down upon them from the plateau. This movement interrupted the communication between our riflemen in the mountains and our main army. No sooner did they discover that the enemy's lancers and infantry had got between them and their friends, than they immediately abandoned their position, and succeeded in forcing their way around the intercepting column below, which for a time was held in check by the Arkansas and Kentucky cavalry, under Colonels Yell and Marshall, who, luckily, had been able to make a short stand after they had gained a little plain [6] in rear of the ravine from which they had just been compelled to retire. In this movement the riflemen suffered great loss, — the Texan company being nearly destroyed. The rest of General Ampudia's force poured down the mountain in hot pursuit, and, uniting with the lancers, compelled the Arkansas men, Kentuckians, riflemen, and all, to give way before them; the two former alternately yielding and disputing the ground, the others following in the footsteps of the volunteers who had first retreated.

Our whole left had now been forced, and the enemy was in possession of every advantage arising from the peculiar nature of the ground; the alternate ridges and ravines being as much in his favor as in ours.

It was at this critical juncture that General Taylor arrived upon the field* from Saltillo, having completed his dispositions for the defence of the city. He was accompanied by Lieutenant-Colonel May, with the two companies of the 2d Dragoons, and by Colonel Davis, with eight companies of his Mississippi riflemen. Captain Albert Pike, with his own company and that of Captain John Preston, Jr. (the two united as a squadron), and Lieutenant Kilburn, with one piece from Captain Bragg's Battery, had also been ordered to the field of battle from below the city, where they had been on detached duty. The Mississippi riflemen halted near the hacienda long enough for the men to fill their canteens with water, when they were turned off from the road diagonally to the left, and advanced toward the point where our troops were fast giving ground to the enemy. The General commanding proceeded on directly to the plateau, having with him the 2d Dragoons.

Up to this time General Wool, being next in command, had assigned the positions for

---

* For the position he assumed, see the Plan of the Battle.

BATTLE OF BUENA VISTA. 73

all the troops, and conducted the battle from the beginning; but, the moment General Taylor arrived at the front and assumed the direction of affairs, he immediately started to assist General Lane in rallying the 2d Indiana Volunteers, and to endeavor to restore something like order to our left, which by this time had swung around so as to face toward the mountains on that side, and in a direction perpendicular to the original line. The position of the batteries still in active operation on the plateau, the point of land on which Colonel Hardin had thrown up a parapet, and Captain Washington's position at La Angostura, were at this moment the only portions of the ground we first occupied, from which we had not been driven. Already our loss in officers and men had been immense; and among them was included the gallant and chivalrous Assistant Adjutant-General, Captain George Lincoln,* one of the most promising young officers in the army, and one who, possessing

---

* He had been endeavoring to rally the 2d Indiana Volunteers, by urging them, by every thing men can hold dear, to return to their duty. Finding all his appeals of no avail, he returned himself to the conflict upon the plateau, when, just as he arrived at the rear of the 2d Kentucky Volunteers, then manfully struggling with the

every quality which can adorn a gentleman, was admired and beloved by all who knew him.

The aspect of affairs was now most gloomy, and our condition most critical; the scale for a short time appeared to be preponderating against us, and Victory to be deserting our banners and winging her way toward those of the enemy. But the idea of yielding the day so long as there was a man left to fight, never, for a moment, came into the mind of our determined leader; and, in his indomitable resolution to compel fortune to favor our side, he was seconded by men, true as the steel they wore, and firm and unyielding as the mountains around them.

The gallant Colonel Davis, with his glorious Mississippians, — men who had been tried in the fire of the storming of Monterey, and had stood the test like pure gold, — now moved steadily forward through the broad current of our retreating horse and foot. He called loudly on those who were flying to come back with him and renew the combat. They were few

---

enemy, he was shot in two places, and instantly expired. Alas! how many were the hearts which the intelligence of his early death penetrated with the deepest sorrow!

BATTLE OF BUENA VISTA. 75

indeed who heeded his call. Colonel Bowles, who, for some reason other than lack of courage, had ordered his regiment to retreat, now, having lost all hope of rallying it again, seized a rifle, and, followed by a handful of his men, joined the Mississippians as a private. During the whole day, he shared their perils, and was distinguished for his personal bravery. With these exceptions, Colonel Davis's appeal was of no avail. In vain he told them, that his riflemen were "a mass of men behind which they could take shelter and securely form." He pointed to his regiment, as he said this. It was indeed a wall of heroes. What must have been his pride in commanding such men! What the mortification and burning shame of the fugitives whom he addressed!

Colonel Davis, as he passed by General Wool, who had now arrived at this part of the ground, was promised support; and the General immediately went in person to hasten the Third Indiana Regiment, from the rear of La Angostura, to his aid. But still the Mississippians moved onward. A large and deep ravine passed by their right, while another entered this after coming diagonally across their front from the left; the two embracing between them an inclined plane, which terminated at a point near their junction (at this moment but a short distance in advance of the regiment), but which was quite broad, and easy to be gained, at its upper and farther extremity near the mountains. On this plane,[8] most of Ampudia's light division was now moving down, flanked by cavalry, and supported by reserves of the heavy infantry.* The 3d Indiana Volunteers had not yet had time to come up, and it was all-important that the enemy should be checked, before he could effect a passage of the only ravine which would seriously retard his course onward to the road. Flushed with success, and apparently irresistible in numbers, he came down like an avalanche. Then it was that Davis and his followers surpassed all their former brilliant efforts. They counted not the odds,— they waited for no support; but, thrown rapidly into order of battle, they pressed forward like Spartans; and, although the air was filled with the sharp hissing of a shower of lead, which came hurtling on, and cutting through their ranks with dreadful effect, still they did

---

* The same that, before day, had reënforced it against our riflemen.

not pause until they had brought the enemy within close range of their own unerring weapons. Then their little line blazed forth a sheet of fire. The shock given by it to the head of the enemy's column was most awful. Men went down before it as ripe grain falls before the reaper. Still the enemy came onward over his dead, and still forward pressed the riflemen, — the latter a handful, the former a host. At length they paused; the Mississippians on the brink of the ravine,[9] the Mexican light infantry on the plane beyond, — the cavalry having been driven to cover on their left. But there was no cessation in the struggle, and Death still continued to gather in his bloody harvest. It was not enough for the Mississippians simply to hold such masses at bay; their blood was up, and the flight of the enemy alone could satisfy them. Giving one loud yell of defiance, which rang on the ear more like the roar of angry lions than the shout of men, they again rushed forward. A moment, and they were lost from the view of their antagonists. It was only a moment; but in it they had dashed into the ravine, clambered up the opposing wall, and now stood before the Mexicans upon their own side. For a few minutes more, the carnage was terrible. At length, bloody and torn, the column of Ampudia lost its steadiness; its fire slackened; then all organization was gone; its ranks were resolved into a confused multitude, which in a moment crumbled away, the whole fleeing precipitately back to the reserves.

The Mississippians then turned to the right, to beat up the cover of what had been the flanking cavalry of this column. They found it attempting to cross the ravine on that hand, in order to attack them in reverse. A few only had crossed, — their commander among them, — but they never went back; and those who were pressing down to succeed them, received a fire it was impossible for them to withstand. They, too, gave way, and fled back to the point whither the light infantry had retreated, and where they were now just forming again.

For a little while, this part of the field appeared to be comparatively safe, and, by the determined valor of one small regiment, an imminent peril to our whole army seemed to be averted. The Mississippians gathered up their wounded, and, taking them to the rear of the first ravine they had crossed, there formed again in line of battle. They were then joined by the 3d Indiana Volunteers, under Colonel Lane, and by Lieutenant Kilburn with one piece of artillery. The fire of this combined force caused those who had just before contended with Colonel Davis's regiment to fall back, for a short time, still farther, and beyond range.

While all this was doing, other large masses of the enemy's cavalry[10] had kept along under the base of the mountains, farther toward Saltillo, and, having crossed many difficult ravines near their sources, moved down directly toward Buena Vista, passing, however, more than half a mile to the right of General Ampudia's column. They had in front of them Colonel Yell's and Colonel Marshall's Mounted Volunteers;[11] too few to offer successful resistance, yet endeavoring to maintain, point after point, the ground they were forced to yield.* Seeing this, General Taylor ordered the handful of cavalry, then near him on the plateau, to move rapidly to the rear, in order to assist in repelling this force. It was all united

---

* Had the Arkansas and Kentucky (mounted) volunteers never been allowed horses, they would have been able to make a stand, on this occasion, as well as the Mississippians.

in one column, under Brevet Lieutenant-Colonel May, and was composed of four companies of regular Dragoons, viz. one under Lieutenant Rucker, assisted by Lieutenant Buford, one under Lieutenant Carleton, assisted by Lieutenant Whittlesey and Lieutenant Evans, one under Lieutenant Campbell, and one under Lieutenant Givens; besides Captain Pike's and Captain Preston's companies of Arkansas Mounted Volunteers. This column moved to the left, passing some distance in rear of the Mississippi regiment, and then established itself on the right of Colonel Marshall's men; Colonel Yell, with his, being on the left. The force, thus accumulated, immediately stopped the enemy, and caused him to fall back again near the mountains. As he could not now be reached by our Dragoons, except in detail, owing to the impossibility of crossing several intervening ravines, otherwise than by one or two paths only wide enough for one horse to pass at a time, Colonel May despatched Lieutenant Evans, of the 1st Dragoons, with a message to General Taylor, requesting some pieces of artillery.

While our cavalry force was thus holding that of the enemy in check, and while the Mississippi Riflemen, and 3d Indiana Volun-

BATTLE OF BUENA VISTA. 81

teers, assisted by Lieutenant Kilburn, were engaged with the troops under General Ampudia, General Wool was making every effort to rally our men who had first given way; and General Lane, though wounded and bleeding, was also endeavoring to gather up the scattered fragments of the regiment with which he had opened the battle. In this they were ably assisted by Inspector-General Churchill, — by Major Monroe, of the Artillery, — and likewise by Captain Steen, of the 1st Dragoons, who fell, severely wounded, while on this duty. None, however, were so successful in arresting their flight, as the intrepid Major Dix, of the Pay Department. Having ridden rapidly in amongst them, he seized the standard of the 2d Indiana Volunteers, and then called to the men, and asked them if they would desert their colors. He told them that they had sworn to protect them, and now, if they were still determined to do so, they must return with him to the fight. He swore to them, that, with God's help, he would not see the state of Indiana disgraced by having her flag carried out of battle until it could be carried out in triumph; and that back into it again it should go, if he had to take it there and defend it alone. This touched the hearts of many of those who were within the sound of his voice. It seemed to banish the panic which had fallen upon them; they were themselves again; they rallied, thought of their homes, gave three cheers for Indiana, and again gathered around her flag. Captain Linnard, of the Topographical Engineers, who had been very active in seconding Major Dix in his appeal to these men, and in putting them in order as they came together, now got a drum and fife, and directed the national quickstep to be played, when the word was given to move on. Major Dix then led off with the flag, while the gallant Captain brought up the rear; and in this way, taking a direction toward Colonel Davis's and Colonel Lane's regiments, back again they went into battle.* All the rest continued their flight; most of them to the hacienda of Buena Vista, but many even to the city of Saltillo, where they reported that all was lost, and our army in full retreat. The reader should bear in mind, that, while all this was taking place to the left and rear, the battle raged with desperate fury on the plateau. This great centre of the conflict was now under the eye and immediate direc-

---

* See Appendix, D.

tion of the respective commanders of the two opposing armies.

Santa Anna, finding it was impossible for the infantry of his centre column to drive back our line of artillery under Sherman and Bragg, and its supporting force under Hardin, Bissell, and McKee, hurried up the Battalion de San Patricio,* with a battery of 18 and 24-pounders; and, with incredible exertions, he succeeded in bringing it around the heads of the large ravine in front, and along the steep sides of the spurs of the mountain, where the battle first opened, and thence down to the very point (L) occupied by O'Brien's section before he moved forward in the morning. Its fire now enfiladed the whole plateau; being directed from its upper edge toward the road.

Even with this additional strength, the centre column could not clear the plateau, but was itself compelled to give ground before the

---

* This *Battalion of Saint Patrick* was composed of some of the Irish soldiers who had deserted from the American army and gone over to the enemy. It was commanded by a man named Riley, also a deserter. Subsequently, the whole battalion was taken in one of the battles in front of the city of Mexico, and sixty of them were hung near Chepultepec. The Irishmen in our army, who had remained true to their colors, were the most clamorous for their execution.

withering effects of the iron poured into it by our light artillery. At length, being broken near its centre, one half pushed over the ravine in rear, and in a direction to reënforce the troops under General Ampudia; while the other half, except the corps of Sappers and Miners, which stood firm by the battery, fell back toward the ravine in front, bearing with them Santa Anna himself, whose horse had been shot down under him. The moment this latter half began to move, Hardin, Bissell, and McKee, with their respective commands, dashed gallantly forward to a point within close musket-shot, when they opened their fire, and followed up the enemy with great slaughter until he became covered by the ravine. Being then, in turn, threatened by the cavalry which had flanked General Mora y Villamil's column, they fell back to the heads of the first and second gorges in their rear; Colonel Hardin's command going to the support of Captain Bragg's section, which, in the mean time, had limbered up and come into battery again, far in advance [12] of its first position.

Lieutenant O'Brien had by this time come back on the plateau once more. He had been obliged (not having a single cannoneer to work the guns) to go down to La Angostura with the section he had been able to bring off, in order to procure a fresh one of two 6-pounders, which Captain Washington gave him in exchange ; and, although Lieutenant French, in consequence of his wound, had been compelled to give up the command of his gun, it fell into good hands, and was kept actively employed under the direction of Lieutenant Garnett, one of the aides-de-camp of General Taylor. So that there were now eight pieces on the plateau alone.

As our left was now the most seriously menaced, not only by the forces which had turned it in the beginning of the battle, but likewise by more than half of the enemy's centre column, General Taylor ordered Captain Sherman and Captain Bragg, each with a section of his battery, to proceed there and strengthen it. This left on the plateau Lieutenant O'Brien with his two pieces, and Lieutenants Thomas and Garnett, each with one. As occasion seemed to render it necessary, the fire of these four guns was directed, now toward the front, now toward the battery at the head of the plateau, and now toward the heavy masses threatening our left and rear, and always with marked effect.

The position of affairs was at this time, in brief, as follows:

The enemy's reserve kept its ground in front. His battery near the road, and likewise his 8-pounder battery, still continued to play respectively upon Washington at La Angostura, and upon the plateau. The third gorge and the ravine in front of the plateau were filled by his first and a part of his second columns of attack, held in check by the 1st and 2d Illinois Volunteers and the 2d Kentucky Regiment, stationed in and near the heads of the first and second gorges, and supporting the four pieces under O'Brien, Thomas, and Garnett. These pieces had the enemy's 18 and 24-pounder battery directly opposite to them, and still close under the mountain at the head of the plateau.[L] The rest of the enemy's second column, all of his third, and the heavy bodies of his cavalry which had turned our left, stretched along near the base of the mountains on that flank, in an irregular line, and faced toward the road; the infantry and a portion of the cavalry were upon the left,[13] nearest the plateau; while the most of the cavalry and a small portion of the infantry were on the right,[14] and nearly opposite Buena Vista. Against this latter part of the enemy's forces, we had also an irregular line. The right of it was composed of the pieces[15] under Sherman, Bragg, Reynolds, and Kilburn, scattered along at uncertain intervals, and having, as their nearest support, Colonel Davis's and Colonel Lane's regiments, together with such of the volunteers of other corps, whether of horse or of foot, as had up to this time been rallied and brought back into the battle. The left[11] consisted of the four companies of the 1st and 2d Dragoons, Pike's and Preston's companies, all that remained of Colonel Marshall's mounted men, and also the fragment of Colonel Yell's regiment, which was on the extreme left.

Following up these various positions, the reader cannot fail to observe, that the whole scene of combat now extended over a space of ground upwards of two miles in length, by nearly a mile in breadth.

For a long while the conflict was continued without any decided success on the part of either army; and the whole field, during this period, might be compared to an intricate game of chess, the Pass at La Angostura, defended by Washington, being the key to our position. If this were carried, we were irretrievably checkmated, and the game was lost.

Had the enemy at this time brought up his powerful reserve, and gathered around it the scattered portions of his first column, it would have required all our artillery under Sherman, Bragg, and O'Brien, and the infantry then on the plateau, to maintain it; while his superiority in numbers in rear might, probably would, have beaten our forces there, and then been at liberty to overpower Washington by attacking him in reverse, or to move on, carry Saltillo, and get possession of all our stores and ammunition there; either of which movements would eventually have destroyed us. But from some unaccountable motive, or blind fatality, he allowed most of his army, still in our front, to remain comparatively inactive; and that too, in one of the most critical conditions of the battle. By doing this, he allowed General Taylor time and opportunity to strengthen his left with artillery from the plateau. The latter promptly seized the great advantage afforded by this fault, as has already been shown; and now, for a season, the balance preponderated slightly in our favor.

About twelve o'clock at noon, Colonel May's

BATTLE OF BUENA VISTA. 89

column of Dragoons was ordered to return from the left to the plateau. Large masses of the enemy's line, extending along the base of the mountain, soon afterward began to give way before the destructive artillery fire, then concentrated upon it, and the determined resistance of the Mississippi Riflemen and the 3d Indiana Volunteers. Some of their corps now attempted to return to the main army in front. Seeing this, General Taylor detached the two companies of the 1st Dragoons, to proceed up the deep ravine [16] in rear of the plateau, and there to charge into and disperse them. These companies had hardly started on this service, before it was observed that a brigade of the enemy's cavalry, mostly lancers, had succeeded in crossing the difficult ravines which lay between it and the Arkansas and Kentucky Mounted Volunteers, and, having forced the latter to give ground, was evidently meditating a descent upon our baggage train, now parked upon the road a short distance below Buena Vista.* Colonel May, with the two com-

---

* It will be remembered that this train, during the night of the 22d, was parked in a hollow, half way from the hacienda to La Angostura. When our left gave way, on the morning of the 23d, the poor teamsters thought

panies of 2d Dragoons, Pike's squadron, and two * pieces of artillery, under Lieutenant Reynolds, was ordered by General Taylor to proceed rapidly to the rear to support that point. This force had hardly started, before it was discovered that the two companies of the 1st Dragoons, which had proceeded toward the mountains on the left, had come under a most withering fire of grape and canister from the 18 and 24-pounder battery [L] at the head of the plateau, which effectually covered the retreat of the corps they went to disperse. General Taylor, therefore, caused them to be recalled. In coming down the plateau to the position the General occupied, they moved directly in front of the whole battery, and besides had a cross-fire of infantry on their left flank. Many of their men and horses

---

the whole army defeated, and in full retreat. They, therefore, started for the city, as fast as their mules could run. It was with the utmost exertion that Captain W. W. Chapman, Assistant Quarter-Master and Aide to General Wool, could stop them. He succeeded, however, in doing so, and in parking the wagons about half a mile below Buena Vista.

* Both belonging to Sherman's Battery; the howitzer which French had, and which Lieutenant Garnett afterwards commanded temporarily, being one. This left only three upon the plateau; — two under O'Brien, and one under Thomas.

were cut up, and their guidon was shot away; fortunately, however, it was soon afterwards recovered. Running the gantlet of such an immense force, the wonder was how these two little companies escaped annihilation. They were immediately ordered to join Colonel May again, to resist the attack threatened on the dépôt at Buena Vista, and on the train; and they proceeded at a gallop for that point, overtaking Lieutenant Reynolds, with his two pieces, on the way. But, before any of this force could reach the extreme left, the brigade of the enemy's cavalry, in column of squadrons,[17] charged furiously into the Arkansas and Kentucky Mounted Volunteers,[18] who had formed a line near the spring in front of the hacienda. The latter had waited until the enemy came within sixty yards, when they fired with their carbines, but with very trifling effect. By the time their pieces were dropped and their sabres drawn, the enemy was amongst them with his lances. The mêlée was then general; the Americans and Mexicans were mixed up in utter confusion, the whole being enveloped in a cloud of dust, and driving on toward the hacienda. Fortunately, the very men who had run off from the field, and had gone to

Buena Vista for shelter, had been gathered up by Major Monroe, assisted by some volunteer officers (Major Trail and Major Gorman among the number), and had been placed on the tops of the buildings, and in a large yard surrounded by a thick adobe wall. They opened a fire upon the Mexican brigade, the moment it had got within range of their muskets and rifles, which killed and wounded a great number. The brigade then divided; one half, mixed up with Arkansas and Kentucky men, went pouring through the narrow street which separates the buildings of the hacienda, while the other commenced falling rapidly back toward the mountains on our left. Lieutenant Reynolds, being now near enough to reach the men of this latter half, came into action; and, having thrown a few spherical-case shot directly into the midst of them, he soon drove them beyond range. He limbered up, and pushed on to the hacienda. The Dragoons under May, and the 1st Dragoons, had arrived there a few minutes before him, but too late to strike the enemy. Those who had fallen back toward the mountains on the left of the Pass were beyond reach, and those who had gone through the hacienda had by this time got separated from the Arkansas and Kentucky men, and had gained the lower level across the stream. Although distant, they were not out of reach of Lieutenant Reynolds's guns. He had brought his section into battery just below the hacienda; and, until they had crossed the whole lower level, and had succeeded in climbing the opposite mountain, and finally in escaping through a small notch near its summit, he continued to play upon them with astonishing accuracy and great execution.

In this affair, our mounted volunteers behaved as well as could have been expected, and suffered much less, considering all the circumstances, than could have been imagined possible. The brigade that charged them, one of the best in the Mexican army, was commanded by General Torrejon, and led on by him in person. It numbered about one thousand; while all that were left, at this time, of the Arkansas and Kentucky regiments could not have been over four hundred and fifty. It was in this charge that the gallant and distinguished Colonel Yell lost his life. He fell like a hero, far in advance of his men, and pierced with many wounds.

Captain Porter, of his regiment, a brave man and most amiable gentleman, died by his side; and Adjutant Vaughn, one of the most promising of the young men of Kentucky and the favorite of his regiment, also fell, fighting to the last. He received twenty-four wounds. Besides these, there were many of the best men of the two regiments killed or wounded. General Torrejon was wounded in this charge, and left thirty-five of his men dead upon the field. The number of his wounded was not known, as their comrades bore them away.

After the Mexicans had failed in their attack on Buena Vista, they made a determined effort to force their way to the road at a point nearer the plateau. They brought down, from near the mountains opposite and to the left of the hacienda, a fresh brigade of cavalry, covered by infantry in all its passages of ravines. With this they advanced to engage the Mississippi riflemen, the fragment of the 2d Indiana Volunteers, and the 3d regiment of the same, who were still acting together, and who had near them one howitzer under Captain Sherman. The position [19] of these troops was some five hundred yards nearer the road than the point where Colonel Davis's regiment was

first engaged in the morning, but farther down
the same ravine. As soon as this new brigade
indicated, by the manner of its approach, its
determination to charge our riflemen and infantry, they were rapidly formed to receive it.
The Mississippi regiment, in line of battle, extended across the little plain upon which they
now were, — their right being near the ravine,
their front toward the mountains; the Indiana troops were formed so that their left rested
on the right of Colonel Davis's regiment, their
right upon the ravine higher up, their front
being also toward the mountains, but more to
the north. In this way, an obtuse reëntering
angle was presented towards the approaching
cavalry, Sherman's howitzer being on its left.
The enemy was formed in close column of
squadrons, and came down the slope at an
easy hand-gallop. His ranks were well closed,
his troopers riding knee to knee, and dressing
handsomely on their guides. All the flags and
pennons were flying, — some fifteen hundred
of them ; — the men were in full uniform, and
the horses elegantly caparisoned. Every lancer
sat erect, and kept his charger well in hand ;
and the whole brigade, preserving exactly its
intervals and the direction of its march, moved

forward with the ease and regularity of the best drilled troops on a field-day. Had the commander of this beautiful brigade desired to win the applause of both armies, he could not have put it in better order, or led his men on with more of professional style. The *tout ensemble* of his column was most admirable. It had a sort of air about it,— an easy, nonchalant manner of going into the work, — which could not but recall to one's mind his ideal pictures of the cavalry of the olden days. Those fine fellows were the chivalry of Mexico, and, with the exception of the President's personal guard, — the regiment of Hussars, — they were the most dashing troops the Republic had ever sent to the field. Opposed to them were our men on foot, — a mere handful in comparison, and having about them none of the "pomp and circumstance," the glitter, and gold, and feathers, and tassels, of their antagonists. They stood calmly and fearlessly still, with their pieces at a carry. But they, too, had an air; one that had mischief in it. Their ranks had been thinned out; some of their best men had fallen. There were even fathers standing there, whose sons had gone down by their sides, — their pet boys, whom they had reared and brought forth to fight for their country. And there were sons, too, whose clothes had been baptized with their fathers' blood, not yet dry. Brothers, who had stood shoulder to shoulder in the morning, stood so no more; but, while one lay stark and motionless upon the earth, the other was near by to avenge him. There were neighbors, too, and friends, who had grown up together in school-boy days. They were not yet separated. The survivors stood there, while those who had borne all these tender relations to them were strown, dead or dying, on every hand. Yet all in sight they lay;— the familiar forms and faces of those to whom they had been deeply attached, and whom they had called by their first names from infancy. It cannot be wondered, then, that these men stood firm.

It was a sublime, a terrible sight. The troops on both sides were so cool and determined, that all knew the struggle must be sanguinary and desperate in the extreme. Not a word was spoken; the din of the surrounding battle seemed for a moment hushed; the rumbling sound of the earth, as the brigade swept onward like a living thunderbolt, appeared to be the only audible manifestation of the approaching carnage. As the Mexicans came nearer, they evidently indulged the belief, that they could draw the fire of our men before it could be very destructive; and that then, while the pieces were empty, they could overwhelm the slight barrier before them, and finish their work with the lance. But finding, on the contrary, that not a piece was discharged nor a man moving, the whole brigade began instinctively to diminish its gait. This was a fatal mistake; and, on their side, it seemed a pity it should have been made, it was so out of keeping with the skill indicated by their soldierly appearance and gallant bearing. Finally, instead of dashing forward in a most splendid charge, as they could have done, having the ground upon which to execute it, they had the madness to pull up to a walk, and at length *to halt* in the very net-work of the two lines of fire. The instant they did so, the pieces came down on both faces of the angle, as if swayed by the same hand. For a moment their muzzles moved slowly about, as each man felt for his aim; then they settled steady and firm as bars of steel. Now, like the blast of a trumpet, the dreadful word was shouted, — " Fire!" Two sheets of flame converged on that beautiful brigade. It was appalling! The whole head of the column was prostrated, and riderless horses, a multitude, and crimson with blood, scattered from it in every direction.

Before the Mexicans could recover from the effects of this blow, Sherman cut them up with grape and canister. Then came the rapid and deadly firing by file, of our riflemen and infantry. No troops in the world could have faced it without the most awful sacrifice of life; and under it the whole brigade gave way, and fled toward the mountains, leaving the ground literally covered with its dead.

In this affair, had it not been for that unaccountable and suicidal pulling up to a halt before a body of the best marksmen in the world, and distant only eighty yards; — had this compact mass of cavalry, in room of doing thus, dashed at speed into the angle before them, they would have lost many men, no doubt; but it is difficult to conceive what could have saved the Mississippi and Indiana troops from total destruction. And, had so large a force broken through our lines, and, at this time, gained the road between Buena Vista and La Angostura, the fortunes of the day would again have been placed in a jeopardy most painful to contemplate.

All this time the fighting on the plateau was continued with but slight intermissions, yet without any important advantage being gained by either side. The enemy's batteries in front, except at short intervals, kept busily at work; but our men at La Angostura, and in the heads of the gorges, sheltered themselves as much as possible, except when the infantry or cavalry would come within range; then, for a season, the sharp roll of musketry would be mingled with the booming sound of cannon, but would again subside to the frequent dropping shot, as the enemy slowly fell back to cover. It was on such occasions, that loaded wagons came along near those regiments and corps which, for the moment, might not be hotly engaged; and, having supplied the men with ammunition and bread and water, took in all the wounded who could be gathered up, and returned with them to the rear. By causing the men, when opportunity offered, thus to be refreshed, and to have their cartridge-boxes replenished, the General was enabled to keep them in a condition to bear their heavy fatigue, and, at the same time, in a good state of preparation for a protracted

BATTLE OF BUENA VISTA. 101

use of their weapons. Besides, in this way the wounded were cared for without taking the combatants from the lines.

But the most sanguinary part of the field was still that which was covered by the forces engaged in rear of the plateau. After the enemy's brigade of cavalry had been repulsed by the artillery, riflemen, and infantry, under Sherman, Davis, and Lane, very soon the companies of the 1st and 2d Dragoons, Lieutenant Reynolds with his two pieces, Pike's and Preston's companies, and a few mounted and foot volunteers who had been rallied at the hacienda, were ordered by General Taylor to move directly up near the base of the mountains on the left, and to drive in the enemy's right by attacking him on that flank. This force was under the direction of Brevet Lieutenant-Colonel May. The Mexicans soon began to give way before its advance, and to keep along the base of the mountain toward the plateau. It was while this was doing, that a violent tempest of hail and rain, with gusts of wind, came suddenly up, accompanied by vivid lightning and the most deafening peals of thunder.*

---

* There was something remarkable about this sudden and furious tempest. It was in the " dry season "; and,

But the warring of the elements above stayed not the fury of the battle below. The loud thunder and the pattering of hail were answered back by the roar of cannon and the rattling of musketry.

From time to time, as our cavalry force under Lieutenant-Colonel May pressed heavily on the right flank of the enemy, Reynolds's two pieces were brought into action, and played upon him until he gave ground, when they were quickly limbered up, and moved on again to new and closer positions; being supported on each flank by the regular Dragoons, with Pike's squadron to the left of all. Meanwhile Captain Bragg, with three * pieces of his battery without support, advanced upon the enemy, midway between the Dragoons and the Mississippi and Indiana troops. The latter were also pushing on, and supporting, as they did so, Captain Sherman with his howitzer.

---

save the slight shower during the night succeeding the battle of the 22d, we had had no rain before, and we had none for a long time after. Some of our army accounted for it as being the result of the excessive firing during the action. According to Professor Espy's theory of storms, this may have been the cause.

* By this time Lieutenant Kilburn's piece had joined him.

BATTLE OF BUENA VISTA. 103

Our three pieces on the plateau likewise directed, for the time being, their fire upon the masses now giving way before this combined attack and advance of our entire strength in rear of that position. Meanwhile the whole fire of the 18 and 24-pounder battery of the enemy was concentrated on our corps moving up toward the mountains, and nearly enfiladed their lines. It was a fine battery, and the havoc it made in our ranks was a melancholy evidence of the skill with which it was served. But neither the effect of its heavy copper-shot, frightful as it was, nor the continuous fire of musketry from those now falling back, could retard the steady advance of our troops. They swept onward toward the mountains like a seine, and gathered this portion of the enemy's force into a sort of *cul-de-sac*, from which it seemed impossible for it to escape. The Mexicans, who were thus hemmed in, were played upon by no less than nine pieces of our light artillery at the same moment; being the centre of a cross fire from Reynolds's pieces to their right, and O'Brien's and Thomas's pieces on their left, while Sherman and Bragg were tearing them up in front. Although at first they answered our troops by a fire of musketry, as the ground from point to point afforded them cover, yet, as they became more condensed, and the effect of our shot more destructive, they grew panic-stricken. Then horse and foot mingled together, and, without pausing to resist the storm under which they suffered, pressed on closer and closer toward the mountain. These were the men who had killed our wounded, when they drove us in the morning. These were the men who took no prisoners, when they might have taken many. These were the men who left no sign of life in any thing American which had fallen into their hands, — the men who had stripped our poor fellows, and then stood over them and mutilated their remains in the most horrible and revolting manner. They were the men who had received the surrendered sword of the Texan Lieutenant, Campbell, a gallant gentleman, and then plunged it into his bosom. These were the men who in the morning had surrounded that grey-haired man, Lieutenant Price, of Illinois, seventy-two years old,* and

---

* This old gentleman had been very active in raising a company of the 2d Illinois Volunteers, by urging the young men of his county to go to Mexico and assist General Taylor, who, he had heard, was surrounded. At last

BATTLE OF BUENA VISTA. 105

cruelly forced their lances through him, as if for pastime. Now they were going back over the same ground where all this work had been done. We had but little consideration for those who had had no pity for our mangled and bleeding comrades. And every one knew, if the battle finally went against us, what would inevitably be his own fate. All these things inspired our troops with a determination never to despair of victory; and nerved them to press onward to the punishment of an enemy, who, in civilized warfare, had set the first example of murdering wounded men. Faster and faster our troops gathered them into that little cove in the side of the mountain. They were about 5000 or 6000 in all; cavalry and infantry, mingled in confusion; an armed multitude; a mere chaos of men and horses, and dead and dying, with flags, pennons, lances, and muskets, all mixed up. Hundreds of them endeavored to escape by clambering up the steep sides of the mountains; but most of them

---

he told them, that, to prove that he would not advise them to go where he dared not go himself, if they would give him a commission, so that he could be "mustered in," he would accompany them. They elected him Second Lieutenant, and he fell as above described. He was much beloved, and his fall was deeply lamented.

stood huddled together, while our shot went crashing through them, and our shells likewise, opening for themselves a bloody circle wherever they exploded.

It was at this time that the President of Mexico sent one of his staff officers, under a white flag, with a message to General Taylor, desiring to know what he wanted. General Wool was immediately directed to bear the commanding General's reply to such a singular request; and, at the same time, orders were sent to our batteries to cease firing. General Wool proceeded directly up to the head of the plateau, where, notwithstanding the interchange of flags, the 18 and 24-pounder battery (L) still continued in operation on our troops in rear; but, finding he could not induce the Mexican officers there to cease their fire, he declared the parley at an end, and returned to our lines, without having had an interview with his Excellency. While all this was going on, the whole force which had turned our left succeeded in escaping from its perilous situation. Having recrossed the head of the deep ravine, they passed rapidly along the upper edge of the plateau, and, under cover of their battery there, in

BATTLE OF BUENA VISTA. 107

spite of all our exertions, united again with the main army in front.

Just before they did so, however, and about the time the white flag came in to General Taylor, Santa Anna caused his 8-pounder battery to be moved down to a point nearer the plateau; and his reserves, under General Ortega, were ordered forward, and formed in the same ravine which had been occupied by General Pacheco in the morning. This large body of fresh troops was strengthened by those of the first column of attack, by the Battalion of Leon, and by the Eleventh Regiment of Infantry.* The whole force was then placed under the command of General Perez, and directed to move forward; the cavalry being ordered to its left, to remain under cover until our lines should give way. The approach, concentration, and disposition

---

* "I had ordered the battery of 8-pounders to advance and take the enemy in flank; [?] and that the column of attack, then posted on our left flank, where it had no object of operation, should be transferred to our right, and there be joined by the remains of the Eleventh Regiment, the Battalion of Leon, and the Reserves, and all under the command of Brevet General Don Francisco Perez. I executed this in person, and afterwards sent for General Mora y Villamil, and made him acquainted with my final dispositions." — *Santa Anna's Report of the Battle.*

of this force, could not be seen from any part of the ground we then occupied; therefore its strength, proximity, and the point it menaced, were, for the present, equally unknown. But, to be prepared for any emergency, General Taylor sent orders to the left, the moment the Mexican right had effected its escape from that quarter, for all our troops there to come forward, as quickly as possible, to the plateau. They were now already in motion; our cavalry and artillery being obliged to go nearly down to the road to avoid the ravines, whilst the Mississippi and Indiana troops were moving directly across them.

While the enemy's cavalry and infantry, which our left had thus signally defeated, was moving in retreat along the head of the plateau, O'Brien's and Thomas's pieces were advanced well to the front, and then came into action, and opened a heavy fire on them; and Colonels Hardin, Bissell, and McKee, with their Illinois and Kentucky troops, dashed gallantly forward in hot pursuit. The powerful reserve of the Mexican army was just then emerging from the ravine where it had been organized, and coming forward on the plateau, opposite the head of the third gorge.[Q]

BATTLE OF BUENA VISTA. 109

Those who were giving way rallied quickly upon it; when the whole force, thus increased to over 12,000 men, came forward in a perfect blaze of fire. It was a single column, composed of the best soldiers of the Republic, and having for its advanced battalions the veteran regiments. The Kentucky and Illinois troops were soon obliged to give ground before it, and to seek the shelter of the second gorge.[P] As the Mexicans pressed on, O'Brien and Thomas opened upon them with canister, instead of round and hollow shot. Being very close, the destruction of life, caused by their three pieces, was immense. The advance of this column, however, was not retarded; for they were troops of the old line, and were accustomed to blood. Arriving opposite the head of the second gorge, one half of this column suddenly enveloped it, while the other half pressed on across the plateau, having for the moment nothing to resist them but the three guns in their front. The portion, that was immediately opposed to the Kentucky and Illinois troops, ran down along each side of the gorge in which they had sought shelter, and also circled around its head; and then there was no possible way of escape for them except by its mouth, which opened upon the road. Its sides were steep, — at least, at an angle of forty degrees, — were covered with loose pebbles and stones, and went to a point at the bottom. Down there were our poor fellows, — nearly three regiments of them, — with but little opportunity to load or fire a gun, being hardly able even to keep their feet. Above, the whole edge of the gorge, all the way around, was darkened by the serried masses of the enemy, and was bristling with muskets directed upon the crowd beneath. It was no time to pause; those who were not immediately shot down, rushed on toward the road, their numbers growing less and less as they went; Kentuckians and Illinoians, officers and men, all mixed up in confusion, and all pressing on over the loose pebbles and rolling stones of those shelving, precipitous banks, and having lines and lines of the enemy firing down from each side and in rear, as they went. Just then, the enemy's cavalry, which had gone to the left of the reserve, had come over the spur that divides the mouth of the second gorge [P] from that of the third,[Q] and were now closing up the only door through which there was the least shadow of a chance for their lives. Many of those ahead endeavored to force their way out; but few succeeded; the lancers were fully six to one, and their long weapons were already reeking with blood. It was at this time that those, who were still back in that dreadful gorge, heard, above the din of the musketry and the shouts of the enemy around them, the roar of Washington's Battery. No music could have been more grateful to their ears. A moment only, and the whole opening, where the lancers were busy, rang with the repeated explosions of spherical-case shot. They gave way. The gate, as it were, was clear, and out upon the road a stream of our poor fellows issued. They ran panting down towards the battery, and directly under the flight of iron then passing over their heads into the retreating cavalry. Hardin, McKee, Clay, Willis, Zabriskie, Houghton, — but why go on? It would be a sad task indeed to name over all who fell during this twenty minutes' slaughter. The whole gorge, from the plateau to its mouth, was strewed with our dead; *all* dead; no wounded there, not a man; for the infantry had rushed down the sides, and completed the work with the bayonet.

Simultaneously with all this, the other portion of the enemy's immense force continued to advance diagonally down the plateau, toward the very point occupied by the commanding General. There was nothing to impede their progress but the artillery under Lieutenants O'Brien and Thomas. The former of these officers, with his two pieces, was about a hundred yards to the right and in advance of the latter; and both, though unsupported, fell back no faster than the recoil of their guns would carry them. They knew our troops were hurrying up from the rear, and that, if they could retard the enemy's course but a few minutes longer, the tide of battle, now setting so heavily against us, might once more turn in our favor. Sherman and Bragg were urging on their batteries with whip, spur, and even with drawn sabres; the dragoons were coming on with them; while to the left, Davis and Lane, with their riflemen and infantry, — the men with trailed arms, — were advancing, at a run, over the ridges and ravines; the awful fire of musketry on the plateau, and down around that dismal gorge, proclaiming with fearful eloquence the necessity of their speed. Closer and closer pressed the Mexicans. O'Brien saw, that, if he limbered up in time to save his guns, the enemy would carry the plateau before our other light artillery could get to it; but that, if he stood his ground and fought them until they were lost, there was still a chance remaining to retrieve the fortunes of the day. It was a most critical moment, and his a most perilous situation. On his choice there rested infinite responsibility. His decision, under the circumstances, was stamped with more of heroism than any other one act of the war. HE ELECTED TO LOSE HIS GUNS.

Still onward came the Mexicans. O'Brien's men were fast falling around him; he was himself wounded; already two horses had been killed under him, and the third was bleeding; besides, those attached to his pieces and caissons were nearly all down, and struggling in their harness. He looked back, and saw that the troops in rear were now nearly up, and encouraged his little handful of men to continue their exertions. The cool and intrepid Thomas, on his left, kept busily at his work, and was likewise suffering most terrible loss. Still the Mexicans came on, and were now almost up to the guns, which were pouring into them canisters on canisters of musket balls. No troops could have behaved better than they did. There was no faltering. The wide gaps opened through their ranks were immediately closed up, and the men still pressed on. Now nearly every cannoneer was down. O'Brien looked back once more, and, thank God! Bragg's Battery, which was leading, was just at that moment coming into action; Sherman and the dragoons were following rapidly up, while Davis and Lane were just bringing their riflemen and infantry out of the last deep ravine upon the plateau. His pieces were nearly loaded again; it was slow work, the four or five men about them being so weak from loss of blood. But he was determined to give the Mexicans one more round; and he did so; it was, as one might say, right in their teeth; and then he, and the few crippled fellows who had survived the carnage, hobbled away.*

---

* This was the manner in which Lieutenant O'Brien "turned over" (to use a professional term for the transferring of property from one to another) these two celebrated trophies to the Mexican army. They were afterwards recaptured by the gallant and lamented Captain Simon H. Drum, of the 4th Artillery, at Churubusco. It is somewhat remarkable, that a company of the very regiment to which they belonged should have retaken them.

While those of the Mexican army nearest the guns closed in on them, and, having cut the dead and dying horses clear, limbered up, and then, by hand, rolled the pieces away, the rest continued rapidly on, their speed being now accelerated to a run. Captain Bragg had appealed to General Taylor for support. There was none to give him. That which had been in front the enemy were now cutting to pieces in the gorge to which it had been driven, while that in rear had not yet come up. "MAINTAIN THE POSITION AT EVERY HAZARD," was the order. And nobly was it executed. That magnificent battery,* — which had encountered the enemy in every battle from Palo Alto up, and before which the Mexican ranks had wilted away as if breathed upon by the Angel of Death, — now belched forth a storm of iron and lead, which prostrated every thing in its front. Nothing could withstand its terrible

---

Speaking of the time when they were recovered, General Scott says; "Coming up a little later, I had the happiness to join in the protracted cheers of the gallant 4th on the joyous event; and, indeed, the whole army sympathizes in its just pride and exultation."

* Ringgold's celebrated battery until he fell; then Randolph Ridgely's at Resaca de la Palma and Monterey, till he died; then Bragg's.

fury. In a few moments Sherman placed his battery alongside, and took up the fire; the dragoons were ordered to a position within supporting distance; and, at the same instant, Washington at La Angostura began to tear open the gate of lancers from the gorge below. Davis and Lane, with the Mississippi riflemen and Indiana Volunteers, having come upon the plateau at some distance to the left of the artillery, poured volley after volley into the enemy, striking him in flank, and enfilading his repeated ranks from right to left. The cannonade on both sides was now so incessant, and the roar of musketry so loud and continuous, that it was impossible, above the general clangor and din, to distinguish the report of any single gun. The struggle was most desperate. The whole air vibrated with the rushing current of balls. The Mexicans fought as they had never fought before, and with an utter disregard of life. Our men were falling on every hand. General Taylor himself was in the midst of the hottest of the fight, calmly giving his orders, his clothes torn and riddled with bullets; and, wherever the fury of the battle was greatest, there was General Wool, riding from point to point, encouraging and stimulating the men to still greater exertions. Each moment our fire seemed to grow more and more destructive. At length, the head of the Mexican column began to fall back; not by retreating, but by being shot away. Others pressed on to supply the places of the fallen; but they, too, went down. Finding it utterly impossible, notwithstanding all were advancing, to gain even a rod of ground against such a tempest, the whole column finally faltered a moment, then gave way, and in confusion retreated to the cover of the deep ravine. Not till then did our fire slacken. The smoke, which had enveloped the two armies like a thick veil, then lifted slowly up, and there was the field, blue with the uniforms of the dead!

With the exception of the 18 and 24-pounder battery and its strong supports, still in position at the head of the plateau, the whole Mexican army had now given ground. It had done so under the combined efforts of Washington's guns at La Angostura, and of Sherman's and Bragg's batteries, Davis's riflemen, and Lane's volunteer infantry, on the plain above.

The remains of the Second Illinois Regiment were soon got together after they had arrived near La Angostura from the fatal gorge, and were again brought upon the plateau by the modest and fearless Bissell, and posted on the right of the batteries. Lieutenant-Colonel Weatherford also gathered up the fragments of poor Hardin's regiment, and marched them out to the head of the first gorge. They thus relinquished the parapet they had thrown up, and also the ditch to the right of Washington, to all that were left of the 2d Kentucky Volunteers, who had been brought away from the gorge after McKee and Clay had gone down, and were now commanded by the only surviving field-officer, Major Cary H. Fry, one of the most determined soldiers in the battle.

Captain Bragg at this time advanced his battery, supported by the Mississippians, two or three hundred yards up the plateau, and opened upon the Battalion of San Patricio with its heavy guns and its sustaining force, the corps of Sappers and Miners, now further strengthened by the regiment of Engineers. Captain Sherman likewise pushed his pieces more to the front, and operated in that direction as the enemy from time to time became exposed to his fire. At the same moment, General Taylor directed Lieutenant-Colonel May, with the companies of the 1st and 2d Dragoons, and Pike's and Preston's companies, to move up the ravine toward the left, to prevent the enemy from again getting to our rear by turning that flank.

It was nearly five o'clock in the afternoon when all these dispositions had been made. The great tumult of the battle had just given place to an occasional cannonade, accompanied by a desultory and scattering fire of small arms, when the attention of our army was attracted toward the rear by the heavy report of guns in that direction.

It will be recollected, that, during the 22d, General Miñon with his brigade of cavalry had come into the valley northeast of Saltillo, and had been ordered by Santa Anna to remain there until our troops gave way, then to fall upon them, and cut them up. About twelve o'clock, at noon, on the 23d, a large detachment of this brigade, apparently impatient at waiting for our precipitate retreat, passed along at the foot of the mountains, and ascended into the Pass through a deep ravine at long cannon range southeast from the redoubt. As they did so, and swept around to gain the road between the battle-field and the city, they were opened upon by Captain Webster with his 24-pounder howitzers, and, before they could get beyond the reach of the shells, sustained a slight loss both in men and horses. During the afternoon, this force was followed on the same route by the rest of the brigade, which, when it had united with its advance, halted in one immense column, — the whole being but a little over a mile in front of the town. In this position General Miñon succeeded in intercepting the flight of several of the men who had left the field of battle, and in making them prisoners. The brigade, however, had hardly gained this new position, before Lieutenant Donaldson and Lieutenant Bowen, of Webster's Battery, galloped over to the head-quarter camp, and, in concert with Lieutenant Shover, proposed that Donaldson and Shover, — the former with one of Webster's howitzers, the latter with his 6-pounder gun, — should go out and attack it by themselves, and, if possible, force it from the Pass. It was a bold plan, and one they were the very men, not only to conceive, but to execute. Lieutenant Shover knew, that, if our army in front of Buena Vista had been routed, as the fugitives had reported, a most desperate stand would probably be made in front of the town, and, for the moment, therefore, he did not feel authorized to leave a position which General Taylor had ordered him to defend to the last extremity. But afterwards, when he found that our lines were still maintaining their ground, and that he could then leave the head-quarter camp without so much danger of compromising its safety, he dashed forward with his gun at a gallop, having for a support a promiscuous crowd of mounted and foot volunteers, teamsters, and citizens, whom Paymaster Weston, Mr. Winder, his clerk, and several other spirited gentlemen had gathered up among those who had fled to the town. They were without organization, or even any commander, and followed on after him as best they might, but yelling and whooping most infernally as they went. Lieutenant Donaldson soon got out his 24-pounder howitzer, and in a few minutes formed a junction with Lieutenant Shover, having for his support Captain Wheeler's company of the 2d Illinois Volunteers. During this time, Miñon's brigade had been put in motion, and was now taking a direction evidently to regain the valley from which it had ascended. Lieutenant Shover, being ahead, was the first to bring it within range. He immediately opened upon it, striking the column in flank, and doing much execution. Lieutenant Donaldson, with his howitzer, then came alongside, when they two, thus united, absolutely drove General Miñon's whole command for at least three miles, causing him very considerable loss. At length, as these two determined officers arrived at some mills * near the mountains toward the east, Captain Wheeler's company was advanced as skirmishers, and occupied the buildings and a stone aqueduct which is there; while the two pieces remained in battery, and continued to play on the brigade. General Miñon several times formed some of the squadrons composing the rear of his column, with a view of charging these guns; but the ground was so broken, and the fire so well directed, that he as often relinquished his purpose. Finally, he hurried on, and at length abandoned the Pass entirely, and, descending through the deep ravines, made a rapid retreat to the plain below the town. He continued, as he did so, a long while under the fire of Lieutenant Donaldson's

---

* Arispe's Mills. They are turned by the water of the spring at Buena Vista. It is carried to them by means of a deep ditch or canal, and by aqueducts across the ravines.

howitzer, which was of heavier metal than the gun of his gallant comrade. This was one of the most daring exploits of the day. The communication between the army and the city being now completely opened again, Lieutenent Donaldson and Lieutenant Shover, with their pieces and supports, returned to their respective posts.

Meanwhile, upon the battle-field, the enemy still held the position where he had first established the battery of the Battalion of San Patricio ; and, as the sun settled down still lower in the west, he was seen to move up one or two other regiments, the more certainly to maintain it. As this force could not be driven from the point it occupied, except at a sacrifice we were not in an immediate condition to make, Captain Bragg's battery, accompanied by the Mississippians,* was withdrawn from

---

* Colonel Davis was severely crippled, when he first came under fire in the morning, by a shot through the bones of the arch of one of his feet. He continued, however, to lead his men until the fury of the battle had subsided, when he was forced by the exceedingly painful and dangerous nature of his wound to seek surgical aid. The remains of his gallant regiment fell into good hands. Major Bradford succeeded him in command, — a gentleman always distinguished for his soldierly bearing, and conspicuous in battle for his coolness and utter contempt of danger.

its fire to the foot of the plateau. Captain Sherman still remained at the same advanced point, and still continued to fire upon such portions of the enemy as he could now and then reach with effect. As the sun sank lower and lower, the occasional rattle of musketry gave place to dropping shot, which, in turn, became less and less frequent, and at length entirely ceased. The fire of artillery on both sides had gradually subsided; the sun went down; the heavy and reverberated report of cannon had longer and more uncertain intervals; finally it was hushed; a profound and painful silence succeeded, and again the cold, deepening shadows of evening began silently to steal over the field. The two armies were still there, and were still sternly regarding each other, face to face. They were standing almost upon the same ground where they had respectively stood the night before. But in the Mexican lines we could hear no animated harangue, no responding *vivas*, nor approving cheers; and the night wind brought not to our ears again the witchery of that sweet music. One could hardly realize, as he now looked upon the dark masses of the two armies, that they had been so mingled in bloody strife since last he saw them similarly situated; all was now so calm. Indeed, hardly a sound could be heard, save the occasional dismal flapping of the wings of the fierce zapalotes,* now hovering over the Pass, or the distant and almost human yell of the hungry wolves, answered by others away in the gloomy recesses of the surrounding mountains. They were already beginning to gather in to their horrible repast. And now, scarcely an evidence of the conflict could be seen, except when one took a closer survey of the ground about him. Then, scattered on every hand, how many and many were the dark forms which met his eye of what had been stalwart men and powerful steeds! some lying as if asleep, and some in strange, unnatural postures, with the moonlight resting steadily and cold on the bright points of uniforms and trappings, all still and firm as if they were belted to stone, — not tremulous and moving, as when on breathing, animated beings. These were fearful proofs of the desperate struggle which had gone by. These ghastly figures, with

---

* *Za-pa-lo-te*, a species of vulture with black body and wings. The head, tail, and tips of the wings are white. They fly by night as well as by day, and are very fierce.

the immovable luminous points resting upon them, were the solemn characters, the terrible hieroglyphics, traced upon the field, which, being deciphered amidst the obscurity of night, told in mute but eloquent language how dreadful a day had passed.

So ended the battle of the 23d of February.

Early in the evening every preparation had been made to resist any attack the Mexicans might offer during the night. Along our whole front there was stretched a close chain of sentinels; while, to observe the enemy's movements, should he attempt before morning again to turn our left by infantry along the mountains, a piquet of twenty-five regular dragoons, under Lieutenant Carleton and Lieutenant Givens, was sent far up the ravine in rear of the plateau. At the same time, the mounted companies of Captain Pike and Captain Preston were directed to proceed to an advanced point across the stream,[21] to watch him from that quarter. The remains of the Mississippi regiment were sent in to the head-quarter encampment near Saltillo, while the seven fresh companies stationed in and near the city were ordered to replace them upon the battle-field. Indeed, every arrangement was soon completed for renewing the struggle the coming day. The wounded were all gathered up, and carried to the cathedral in town.* Our troops, without moving from their positions, were supplied with bread, meat, and water; and our dragoon and artillery horses, still under the saddle or in harness, were refreshed with forage where they stood. All these things being done, the night passed slowly away, and, although cloudless, was extremely inclement. The troops were nearly exhausted from their protracted labors; and now, in addition to their fatigue and want of sleep, they were suffering intensely from the cold. It was a most gloomy and horrible night, and one which our soldiers, who stood shivering there amidst the dead, and with their arms in their hands ready

---

* A large train of wagons, filled with our wounded, was conducted to Saltillo, during the night of the 23d, by Enoch C. March, Esq., of Illinois, a most gallant old gentleman, and one who, though connected with the army only in a civil capacity, was always found, during the battle, where he could be of service; whether it was in the thick fight, in gathering up our poor fellows who were mangled and bleeding, in rallying those who had given way, or in the melancholy duty of conducting this long train to the cathedral in the city.

for instant combat, can never forget. No one despaired of ultimate success. The advantages the enemy had at first gained had been, one after another, wrested from him. So far the battle was ours ; and every man upon the field still held firm his resolution that it should continue to be ours. But already seven hundred and forty-six * of our little army had been struck down, and all felt that the anticipated conflict of the approaching morrow would be as bloody as that of the day which had gone. No wonder, then, that this was a most anxious and melancholy night.

During the evening of the 23d, General Marshall, with a battery of four heavy guns under the gallant and accomplished Captain Prentiss of the U. S. 1st Artillery, and a detachment of Kentucky Mounted Volunteers, started from the Pass of the Rinconada, and, by a forced march, succeeded in running the gantlet of Blanco's and Aguierra's rancheros at Capellanía on his right, and General Miñon's whole brigade on his left, and, before morning, arrived within striking distance of Buena Vista. Too much praise could not be bestowed upon this little command for its extraordina-

---
* See Appendix, E.

BATTLE OF BUENA VISTA.

ry efforts to get to the field in time to share in the perils and glory of the conflict. In less than one night, it marched thirty-five miles over one of the worst of roads; and, at the crossing of every ravine, the officers and men were obliged to assist with ropes, not only in letting the cannon down the first bank, but in pulling them up the opposite one. In this way those determined fellows came on, with the enemy, more than ten to one, hovering about them on every hand. The timely approach of this force, together with the troops he had drawn from Saltillo, afforded General Taylor quite as many combatants, in front of Santa Anna, as he had when the battle commenced, and even one piece of artillery more.

At length the long hours of the night had worn slowly away. Just before day, the moon went down. Soon afterward, the gray, and then the purple streaks of morning began to lighten up the eastern sky, and the stars, one by one, to melt into the blue of heaven. Gradually the surrounding objects became more and more distinct as the day approached. Then it was that a sound went along our lines ever to be remembered. It was but a single cry at first; then a murmur, which rose and swelled upon the ear like the voice of a tempest; then a prolonged and thrilling shout:

Victory! Victory! Victory! The enemy has fled! The field is ours!

Reader! you should have heard the wild hurrah that then rang throughout that Pass; the long, exultant, American "Hurrah!" Even the old mountains themselves turned traitors for the moment, and yelled to their hoarse echoes to repeat it. Again and again it sounded, and right over the inanimate remains of the gallant men who had poured out their blood and yielded up their lives to win this new glory for their country. And then, with mingled feelings of sorrow for the dead, joy for the victory, and gratitude to God, many a strong heart was moved; the big drops trickled down many a rough and powder-blackened face; and stern, brave men, whose eyes, for many a long day, had not known the refreshing moisture of a tear, wept now, even while they shouted in triumph.

And it was so; — the heavy masses of the Mexican army, which, when the night shut down, extended along our front from the stream to the mountains, were nowhere to be seen when the coming day again lit up the

Pass. Silently, and almost as unaccountably, as the phantoms of a vision, they had gone away. But, in the twenty-five hundred dead and wounded men,* whom they had left behind, and who would not vanish with the darkness, we had melancholy evidence, that their having been before us, and struggled with us for two long days, was something more real than the flitting vagaries of a dream.

By seven o'clock, our scouts brought the information that Santa Anna's whole army had fallen back on Agua Nueva; but our troops were not only too much exhausted, but too few, to pursue and attack him there. Soon afterwards, General Taylor, accompanied by General Wool and nearly all the staff, and having, as a guard, the companies of the 1st and 2d Dragoons, and Pike's squadron, moved up to the plateau and along over the battlefield; and thence, following the enemy's trail, to La Encantada. No one can imagine, much less describe, how dreadful a scene it was for the whole way. All of our men who had fallen, and whom the enemy had been able to

---

* See Appendix, F.

reach, were stripped of every article of clothing, and gashed over with wounds evidently inflicted after death. The Mexicans, on the contrary, lay just as they had died. The plateau was covered with the dead, and the gorges and ravines in front were filled with them. The ground, furrowed by cannon-shot and torn by the bursting shells, was literally reeking with blood. Men and horses, parts of equipments, shattered muskets, drums, trumpets, lances, swords, caps, — in fine, all the paraphernalia of armies, were scattered, crimson with gore, in every direction. The Mexican wounded had nearly all been taken to the cover of the ravines, or along the road beyond cannon range; and two or three surgeons had been left behind, and were now busily engaged in trying to save them. As our dragoons passed along over this part of the field, the cries for water, which were heard in every direction, were truly heart-rending. Our men dismounted, and gave the poor fellows their canteens, and placed beside them, upon the ground, the contents of their haversacks. It was a touching sight.

Arriving at La Encantada, General Taylor directed Major Bliss, Assistant Adjutant-General, escorted by twenty-five dragoons under Lieutenant Buford, to proceed with a flag to Agua Nueva, and negotiate with General Santa Anna an exchange of prisoners. We had taken nearly three hundred, and it was the General's desire to give them up for those, who, under Major Gaines and Major Borland, had been captured by General Miñon, at Encarnacion, some time before the battle. The Mexican army had taken only seven of our men on the 22d and 23d of February, and those not on the battle-field,—there, they took none,—but between Buena Vista and Saltillo. General Taylor also directed Major Bliss to request the Mexican commander to send for the wounded he had left behind, and to express to him the desire still cherished by the American government for the reëstablishment of peace.

When Major Bliss arrived near Agua Nueva, he was halted by the enemy's guards; but, having made known that the purpose of his visit was to obtain an interview with General Santa Anna, he and his interpreter* were both blindfolded, and were then conducted

---

* Mr. Thomas H. Addicks, of San Antonio de Bexar, Texas.

forward to a room in one of the buildings of the village which had escaped the conflagration. There the bandages were taken from their eyes, when they found themselves in the presence of the Mexican President, surrounded by his generals. The Major at once informed his Excellency of the mission with which he was charged. To this, General Santa Anna, — to use his exact language, as reported by himself, — replied as follows:

"Say to General Taylor, that we sustain the most sacred of causes, — the defence of our territory and the preservation of our nationality and rights; that we are not the aggressors, and that our government has never offended that of the United States. We can say nothing of peace while the Americans are on this side of the Rio Bravo del Norte, or occupy any part of the Mexican territory, or blockade our ports. We are resolved to perish or vindicate our rights. Fortune may not always favor the enemy; his experience on the 22d and 23d should convince him that his luck may change. The Americans wage against us a war of Vandalism, whose excesses outrage those sentiments of humanity which one civilized nation ought to evince toward another. In proof of this assertion, you have but to go outside of this apartment to see still smoking the dwellings of this recently flourishing village; you passed the same vestiges of desolation at La Encantada, on your route hither; and, if you will go a little farther on, there, to Catana, you will hear the moans of the widows and orphans of innocent victims who have been sacrificed without necessity.

"With respect to the wounded whom General Taylor invites me to send for, I can only say there can be none save those who have been too much hurt to arise from the field, or those most in advance who remained in the ravines; and, as I have not the means for their conveyance, I trust that, under the protection of the law of nations, he will have them carried to Saltillo. As for the prisoners General Taylor wishes to exchange, I know not who they can be, unless some of our dispersed troops, or some who, from the fatigue of the last two days, remained asleep when we moved. But, in consideration of the courtesy he has shown with regard to our wounded, I consent, in the name of the nation, to release all the prisoners we have, whether taken at Encarnacion or La Angostura."

His Excellency, in continuation, spoke of his having won the battle of General Taylor, as of something about which there could be no difference of opinion. He remarked casually, that he had brought with him, as trophies from the field, three pieces of ordnance, and as many stands of colors;* and that, in falling back to the position he then occupied, he had done so as a mere matter of convenience to himself and his army. Major Bliss and his interpreter were then permitted to take their leave without being blindfolded. The Major immediately returned, with his escort, to Buena Vista, the commanding General having come back from La Encantada during his absence.

All the rest of the 24th, and the day following, were spent in collecting and burying our dead,† and in gathering up the Mexican

---

* The reader has already been informed how Santa Anna obtained the three cannon to which he alluded. The flags, which he dignified by the title of "stands of colors," were merely the small ensigns which belonged to some of those volunteer companies who ran from the field, and which, being encumbrances to their flight, their bearers had thrown away.

† Each regiment and corps chose for itself some quiet little nook to the left of the small eminence [22] in rear of

wounded, and taking them to Saltillo, where they received precisely the same personal kindness and professional treatment from our surgeons as had been bestowed upon the men of our own army. Preparations were also made to renew the conflict, should the enemy return. Captain Prentiss's heavy guns took the place of Washington's Light Battery at La Angostura; and Lieutenant Benham, of the Engineers, with a large detail of men, soon improved the ditch, raised the epaulment, and strengthened the traverse at that point to such a degree as to make it far more difficult to carry than ever.

Up to this moment, in describing the hurried movements and combat of the two forces, and the continued pressing of one important event upon another, it has been impossible, — without danger of injuring the impression it was hoped the reader would have of the battle in its progress from the beginning, — to mention many individuals by name, except those belonging to the Line of the Army. To all who have thus far perused this narrative, this must certainly have been self-evident.

La Angostura, and there buried, side by side, the remains of the gallant men death had selected from it.

But justice to the Staff, always so distinguished, demands that, at this point, the names of all its members, who participated in the conflicts of the 22d and 23d of February, should be distinctly recorded.

Of the Adjutant-General's Department, there were but two officers on the field; Major Bliss and Captain Lincoln. It would be supererogatory to write here any thing more than the names of these two distinguished soldiers. The same remark is applicable to Inspector-General Churchill, and to Colonel Whiting, Assistant Quartermaster-General, two of the staunchest veterans in the service. Colonel Belknap, on duty in the staff of the commanding General, was conspicuous for his efforts to rally our flying troops, as was also Major Munroe, Chief of Artillery. Major Joseph H. Eaton and Lieutenant Garnett, aides to General Taylor, and Lieutenant McDowell, aide to General Wool, carried the orders of their respective chiefs into all parts of the field, and were noticed everywhere for their coolness and address. The same may be said of Lieutenant Robinson, aide to General Lane. Of the Quartermaster's Department, there were but two captains present;

Captain William W. Chapman and Captain Chilton. The former, as extra aide to General Wool, displayed great bravery in repeatedly conveying orders under the most withering fire, and was highly complimented for his admirable arrangements for the defence of the train on the afternoon of the 23d. The latter, being extra aide to General Taylor, was conspicuous for his daring. Captain Sibley, of the same department, was on duty at the head-quarter encampment near Saltillo, where, though not actively engaged, he rendered good service.

Of the Medical Department, there were on the field Dr. Hitchcock, Dr. Madison, Dr. Levely, and Dr. Prevost. They were ably assisted by the surgeons of the Volunteer regiments. The courageous manner in which these gentlemen passed along our lines and rendered assistance to the wounded, oftentimes at the moment they fell; the positions of imminent peril to which they cheerfully and at all times hurried, whenever their professional services were required on the instant; the care with which they had those who were struck borne to the rear, and subsequently carried to Saltillo, and their assiduity in attending upon them day and night, gained for them the unqualified praise of the whole army. Major Dix, Major Coffee, and Major Colquitt, of the Pay Department, and extra aides to the commanding General, were, in a high degree, conspicuous for their intrepidity.

The services, during the battle, of Major Mansfield, of the Corps of Engineers, were just such as would be expected from an officer who enjoys the reputation throughout the army of being qualified in every respect to command a hundred thousand men. Lieutenant Benham, of the same corps, was always in advanced positions, and consequently always in danger. He performed his duties with great credit, and had the honor to be wounded. Of the Corps of Topographical Engineers, there were five officers present in the battle; Captain Linnard, Lieutenant Sitgreaves, Lieutenant Pope, Lieutenant Franklin, and Lieutenant Bryan; and each one of them was highly distinguished for the fearlessness with which he discharged the important duties of his station. They all served as extra aides to General Taylor or General Wool.

Lieutenant Kingsbury was the only officer of the Ordnance Department present. In addition to the performance of the legitimate and extremely arduous duties of his station, he likewise served as extra aide to the commanding General, and acquitted himself with gallantry. The Subsistence Department was well represented by Captain Amos B. Eaton, who also served upon the field in the immediate staff of General Taylor. Major Craig, Chief of Ordnance, and Surgeon Craig, Medical Director, had been detached from headquarters, and did not arrive upon the field until the morning of the 24th, but came in time to render valuable services in their respective departments of the staff. Major McCulloch, Major Roman, Captain Davis, Captain Howard, Captain Naper, and Captain Gilbert, of the Volunteer staff, did their duty like soldiers. Mr. Thomas L. Crittenden, of Kentucky, volunteered his services as aide to General Taylor. His coolness and daring were the subject of remark. Mr. March, Mr. Parker, Mr. Addicks, Mr. Potts, Mr. Henry A. Harrison, Mr. Burgess, Mr. Henry Howard, and Mr. Dusenbury, though not attached to the army in a military capacity, went upon the ground and fought with great courage.

During the evening of the 25th, Lieutenant

Rucker, with his company of 1st Dragoons as a guard, marched all the Mexican prisoners, who were to be given up, to La Encantada, where Inspector-General Churchill formally turned them over to Captain Faulac of the Mexican army, the Adjutant-General of Santa Anna.* On the 26th, our spies reported that the enemy was beginning to break up his camp at Agua Nueva, and was rapidly falling back upon the road leading toward San Luis de Potosí. Early in the afternoon of that day, a strong party of observation, composed of the two companies of the 1st Dragoons, associated with Pike's and Preston's companies of Arkansas Mounted Volunteers, pushed on within half a mile of Agua Nueva, and, during a close reconnoissance, succeeded in capturing two lancers, from whom it was ascertained that the whole of the enemy's artillery and infantry had already gone, leaving a force of upwards of 3000 cavalry, under General Torrejon, to cover their retreat. On the 27th our entire army returned to Agua Nueva. The enemy's cavalry had abandoned that place at half past eight o'clock in the morning. Our advance-guard, composed of the 1st Dragoons, entered

---

* See Appendix, G.

BATTLE OF BUENA VISTA. 143

it two hours later. The ruins of the village were literally crowded with the enemy's wounded, and many who had died were lying about still unburied. Here we learned from the surgeons and wounded officers, who had been left behind, that the whole Mexican army was in a state of utter disarray and demoralization; that 4000 men, at least, had already deserted, 3000 of them having abandoned their colors on the night of the 23d.* It was General Taylor's purpose at once to pursue the enemy so as to beat up his quarters at Encarnacion by daybreak the following morning; but, upon examination, our cavalry and artillery horses were found to be so exhausted, as to be in no condition to take the road for so long a march without water, until they had had at least one day's repose.

On the 28th, the wounded whom the enemy had abandoned at Agua Nueva were carried to the hospitals at Saltillo. Late in the evening of the same day, the few prisoners General

---

* Which was the fact. We subsequently learned that at least 2000 went by Parras, toward the west; that as many more passed by La Hedionda toward the east; while large numbers took the Mazapil road, and scattered through the country in that direction.

Miñon had taken came in from Encarnacion, having been released at that point by Santa Anna, and furnished with passports to our army. Lieutenant Sturgis and the dragoon, who had been lost at La Hedionda on the evening of the 20th, and whom we had considered as sacrificed, to our astonishment and great joy returned with this party. At the time they were captured, they had arrived at the top of the hill, which they had climbed in order to reconnoitre the valley beyond, when they were fired upon by an out-lying piquet of General Miñon's brigade, some twenty-five in number; but, fortunately, were not struck. They immediately turned and ran down towards the place where they had been obliged to leave their horses, the whole piquet following them. In their rapid flight, they both fell prostrate, and were overtaken and secured by the Mexicans before they could recover their feet. They would have been murdered on the instant, had it not been for the timely intervention of the officer commanding the party. They were then taken to General Miñon's head-quarters at Guachuchil. The General treated Lieutenant Sturgis with marked courtesy and kindness, and showed a most gentlemanly and delicate regard for his situation and feelings; not asking, or permitting any of his officers to ask, any questions about our army, about the immediate purpose of our strong party of observation then at La Hedionda, or any other question which the Lieutenant could not answer with perfect freedom and propriety. He then figured as a mere spectator in the brigade, in its march to the valley north of Saltillo, and, during the battle, in its advance up into the Pass between the city and Buena Vista. All the time it was under the fire of Webster's, Donaldson's, and Shover's guns, he had the misfortune to be in imminent peril of his life from the shot of his most intimate friends, then cutting up the brigade about him. On the morning of the 24th, he still accompanied General Miñon, as he left the valley by the Palomas Pass, and as he afterwards circled around by the way of San Antonio to La Hedionda, and thence, finally, to Encarnacion. On being released at that point, General Miñon kindly presented the Lieutenant with a most beautiful cloak, made of black velvet and richly embroidered; and also with a horse, on which to return to Agua Nueva. Santa Anna likewise gave him a passport under his own hand. Justice toward General Miñon, who is represented as being a most accomplished and elegant gentleman, requires that his kind and considerate deportment toward one of our officers, whom the fortune of war had thrown into his hands, should be fully stated.

On the 1st of March, Colonel Belknap was furnished with a command, and ordered to proceed to Encarnacion to cut up the enemy's rear guard of cavalry, reported as still remaining at that place. This command was composed of the four companies of the 1st and 2d Dragoons; two pieces from Washington's Battery; two or three hundred volunteer cavalry, including Major McCulloch's Texas spy-company, and Colonel Bissell's Second Regiment of Illinois Volunteers; the last in wagons, so as to move rapidly and still be fresh for combat. It left Agua Nueva at three o'clock in the afternoon, the purpose being to march most of the way in the night, the better to elude observation, and then to attack the enemy in his camp at daybreak the following morning. There was every indication, for the whole of the way, of a most hurried retreat and the most dreadful distress. The road was literally strewed with the dead and dying, and with those perishing from fatigue and want of water. It was a most melancholy and touching picture, that of soldiers in uniform, who, having been spared in battle, were now yielding up their lives without a wound.

Colonel Belknap arrived at Encarnacion just at the first gray of morning; but nearly all of the enemy had fled. Several white flags were flying upon the battlements of the church of the hacienda and other elevated points, indicating any thing but resistance on the part of those who still remained. Some few officers and men, on seeing the approach of our party, attempted flight by mounting their horses and hurrying away. The Texas spy-company started in pursuit of them, and, as it was a level and open plain, the whole chase was in full view of the command. The Mexicans, one after another, were caught to a man, and conducted back to the hacienda.

We imagined, that, during the battle, and upon the field when the conflict was ended, and afterwards upon the road over which the enemy had retreated, we had witnessed human suffering in its most distressing forms. But such was not the case. The scene presented to our eyes on entering within the walls of Encarnacion was so filled with extreme and utter agony, that we at once ceased to shudder at the remembrance of any misery we had ever before looked upon. There were three hundred men crowded together in that wretched place, two hundred and twenty-two of whom had been wounded at Buena Vista and brought thus far. There were five officers amongst them. As they had received but little surgical attention, and had been harassed and worn down by travelling so far, while debilitated with pain and loss of blood, their wounds were nearly all either gangrened or highly inflamed. Many of them were enduring the most excruciating torments; many were delirious from excess of anguish; while others, whose wounds had become mortified, were perfectly composed, and yet were even more piteous to behold, as their very quietness was but a more certain indication of speedy dissolution. In fine, the whole hacienda presented, at one glance, a picture of death, embracing all the degrees, from the strong man, bearing up with fortitude against the sure and speedy fate which awaited him, down to the poor mortal struggling in the last throe of existence. And all intermixed with them, were the bodies of those who had just commenced the long journey, yet warm, and lying in the various positions they were severally in when life departed. Poor fellows! No beloved eye had beamed tearfully upon them in their last moments. No voice of affection had murmured in their ear little gentle words of hope, or that touching comfort, "*We shall meet again!*" And there was no kind hand to honor their remains by straightening them for the grave.

During the fury and excitement of battle, we had no time to indulge in feelings of sympathy and commiseration for distress; particularly when we witnessed it among those of our enemies who had been stricken down. Then, we were Americans, and they Mexicans, our bitter and relentless foes. Now, meeting together when the thunder and excitement of the battle had subsided, we were men, and were meeting too on that level, of which all become sensible in the presence of death. The Mexicans had been taught to believe the Americans were almost savages; but, when they saw our men kneeling down beside their suffering comrades, grasping them kindly by the hand, giving them water, and all the bread and meat they had brought for themselves, they were affected even to tears, and feelingly exclaimed, "*Buenos Americanos! Buenos Americanos!*" There was a priest there, dressed in his white robes; and, without exaggeration it may be said, his whole time, while we were there, was occupied in administering the sacrament of extreme unction to those who were dying.

At Encarnacion, we learned that Santa Anna himself had hurried on directly to the capital, but that all that was left of his army, in a state of almost positive disorganization, had retired by the way of Cedral, Vanegas, and Matahuala; General Miñon's brigade covering the retreat. Couriers preceded the President, announcing to the people a brilliant victory over the Americans! * Bonfires and illuminations lit up every town and city from the Gulf of Mexico to the Pacific Ocean. Fêtes and balls, and merry peals of bells, and grand processions and orations, were the consequences of the report of a triumph, which flew throughout the length and breadth of the land. As early as the 27th of February, Santa Anna wrote to the Minister of War and

---

* See Appendix, II.

Marine an account of the operations of his army, and concluded by saying; "The nation, for which a triumph has been gained at the cost of so many sufferings, will learn, that, if we were able to conquer in the midst of so many embarrassments, there will be no doubt as to our final success in the struggle we sustain, if every spirit but rallies to the one sacred object of common defence. The army has done more than could be expected under the laws of nature. After a march of twenty leagues,[!] sixteen of them without water, and without other food than a single ration, which was dealt out at Encarnacion,* it endured the fatigue of combat for two days, and finally triumphed." What a triumph! If the manner in which the Mexican forces retreated from Buena Vista, and went back toward the capital of the Republic, was that which should characterize the return of a victorious army, God spare us from ever winning a battle!

We afterwards learned from the Mexicans themselves, that every hacienda and rancho, on the road over which their countrymen retreated, was crowded with the wounded, and

---

* See Appendix, I.

those who were sick and disabled from the hardships and sufferings incident to such a confused rout; and that, finally, of all that army which, one month before, had left San Luis Potosí, confident of success, and moving off in its strength with inspiring music, with pomp and magnificence, with the brazen clangor of trumpets, and with banners flying, — an army commanded by the President in person, and the finest the Republic had ever sent to the field, — there returned less than 12,000 men, and they worn down by fatigue, with loss of discipline and *morale*, and with all their high bearing completely subdued.

During the night of the 2d of March, Colonel Belknap's command returned to the camp at Agua Nueva. On learning the wretched condition of those of the enemy left at Encarnacion, General Taylor sent to their relief eighteen mule-loads of provisions and other necessaries, and, at the same time, had such of the wounded as were capable of being removed, brought to Saltillo, where they could receive better attention.

While the main "Army of Occupation" was thus employed in the advanced points to which its operations had been pushed, its line of communication with its dépôts of supplies at Camargo, Matamoras, and the Brazos St. Iago, was entirely cut off by the large cavalry force, under General Urrea and General Romero, then on the road between Monterey and the Rio Grande. One of our trains had been attacked, its escort captured, and its unarmed teamsters had been butchered, and then burnt with their wagons. Attempts to destroy several other trains had likewise been made; but the different forces which guarded them had the better fortune to drive the enemy off, and, on two or three occasions, to cause him considerable loss. Now that Santa Anna's principal army had been beaten from our front, it was an easy matter for General Taylor to open his communication to the rear. For this purpose, leaving General Wool in command at Agua Nueva, he started, on the 8th of March, for Monterey, whence, proceeding in person against General Urrea and General Romero, he at once forced them beyond the Sierra Madre, thus leaving the whole valley of the Rio Bravo del Norte again in our possession.

At the Battle of Buena Vista, the conflict

was begun with only 4691 men on the American side. Santa Anna's army numbered more than 21,000, in our front, all regulars; General Miñon's brigade of veteran cavalry of 2000, and the ranchero force at Cappellanía of 1000, in our rear; beside the brigade of General Urrea and General Romero, east of Monterey. The *whole* of this force, reckoning from the Rio Grande, was cut up or driven back far to the south of the mountains, and all by our handful of men, *in less than twenty days* after the first gun was fired.

The effects of the Battle of Buena Vista upon the war were incalculable. Had Santa Anna destroyed General Taylor's army, — and, under the circumstances, defeat and total destruction were synonymous, — he could have poured his triumphant column through that gate of the mountains, the Rinconada Pass, into the valley of the Rio Grande; and then, subsisting upon our stores, fighting with our guns and our ammunition, and using our extensive means of transportation with which to pursue his onward course, what could have interposed to prevent this self-styled "Napoleon of the West" from executing his favorite vaunt, that he would plant the flag of Mexico upon the banks of the Sabine? In addition to all this, Colonel Doniphan's command, which fought the battle of Sacramento on the 28th of February, must inevitably have been cut off, and every advantage, which, from the battle of Palo Alto up to that time, had been won at so much cost of blood and treasure, would have been snatched from us, and the whole war farther removed than ever from any prospect of a termination. Had Santa Anna been victorious over the Americans at Buena Vista, and then pushed his operations into Texas, with a force, it will be remembered, of over 26,000 regulars, well supplied with all the *matériel* of war, would the investment of Vera Cruz have been attempted at the time it was? Would not the veteran army of the United States have been compelled first to retrace its steps in order to force back the veteran army of Mexico?* Suppose Santa Anna had been successful, would he not have had time, had it been his policy so to do, to reach Vera Cruz, and attack General Scott, even before the city and the Castle of San Juan d'Ulloa had surrendered? Or, had he marched directly to Cerro

---

* See Appendix, J.

Gordo, with such an army to oppose the advance of the General-in-Chief to the capital, how immense the force we should have been obliged to send into the field; how great must have been the destruction of life; and what an expense of treasure and of time, too, must there have been, before our flag would have floated, as it now does, above the towers of the ancient city of the Aztecs. Besides, had Santa Anna been successful in his northern campaign, the whole nation would have been animated with enthusiasm, and would have risen in arms. The internal dissensions, by which its energies were paralyzed, would have disappeared. The cries of the numerous parties opposed to the government would at once have been drowned by shouts of triumph. Then, with her population of seven millions, with her *people* united and taking up arms, and with her difficult mountain passes, Mexico would have been a formidable antagonist to any invading army, which should attempt to penetrate to her capital. It needed but one victory to produce this great change. And so the leading men of the country understood it. They had, therefore, spent much time, and exercised great care, in collecting, even from remote states, in organizing, and in preparing at all points, what was called "the Liberating Army of the North." It was composed of the very flower of Mexico, and was commanded by her most distinguished warrior, — the *prestige* of whose name alone was regarded as worth a host. It was a beautiful body of men; the just pride and the hope of every patriot in the land. In a country whose vitals were torn by open rebellion, as well as by the insidious and assassin-like machinations of plotting factions, — without a dollar in her treasury, and with ruined credit, — it had been a great, a most difficult, effort to produce it. It went forth, and the whole nation kept a listening ear turned toward the direction of its march. Each breeze from the north was expected to bear upon its wings a cry of victory. It came at length, and glad sounds, as of a Jubilee, arose from every city and hamlet; but, ere their echoes had died away, the shattered remnant of an army was seen returning; — an army defeated and ruined. It was all that was left of the Liberating Army of the North. The whole Republic comprehended at once the character of the triumph it had just celebrated, and, losing heart, despaired of success from that moment.

Such were the results of the operations of General Taylor's little "Army of Occupation" during one short month.

When the disparity of numbers, — the long time in which the two armies struggled together, — their condition, respectively, as they approached each other, and their comparative condition after they had separated, — are all carefully considered, the Battle of Buena Vista will probably be regarded as the greatest ever fought on this continent; and it may be doubted if there can be found one that surpasses it in the history of any nation or of any age.

APPENDIX.

A.

(See page 35.)

The following letter, descriptive of the marches alluded to in the text, was written by the author of the preceding narrative, for the Washington "Union." As it may be interesting, from the account it gives of the country passed over by the "Centre Division," commanded by General Wool, it is here published at length.

"Camp of the Centre Division, near Parras,
"State of Cohahuila, Mexico, December 13, 1846.

"To the Editor of the Union:

"The numerous correspondents to your paper, who are with General Taylor and General Kearney, have kept your readers well advised of all the transactions of the 'Army of Occupation' and the 'Army of the West,' even to the minutest detail. But the 'Centre Division,' under General Wool, although it has advanced farther into Mexico than either of the other two, has hardly been heard from since the day it passed the Rio Bravo del Norte.

. . . .

"The Centre Division is now within 600 miles of the Pacific Ocean. Its march, since it first passed the natural boundary of the two republics, has been a long and excessively arduous one; and I now devote the first leisure hour I have had for a great while to giving you a brief and hurried account of some of the events which thus far have marked its progress.

"On the 8th of October, the advance of this column, commanded by General Wool in person, and numbering 1954 in the aggregate, arrived on the left bank of the Rio Grande, near the Mexican town San Juan Bautista, better known as Presidio. It had been eleven days in traversing the country from San Antonio de Bexar to that point, a distance of 182 miles. A flying bridge had been constructed by Captain Fraser, of the Engineers, and transported in wagons from San Antonio, for the passage of the river. It was soon put in operation; and, by the evening of the 11th, the whole of the command, and the immense train of stores which accompanied it, were safely landed upon the opposite shore. The Rio Grande at that place was found to be 270 yards wide. Its current was exceedingly rapid, and its waters turbid and of a yellowish-gray color, like those of the Missouri.

"At this point General Wool published an order, in which he defined the course he intended to pursue. He said that he had not come to make war upon the people or peasantry of the country, but to compel the government of Mexico to render justice to the United States. All, therefore, who did not take up arms against us, but remained quiet and peaceable at their homes, he should not molest or interfere with, either as regarded their persons or their property; and all those who should furnish supplies would be treated kindly, and be liberally paid for whatever we should receive from them.

"The better to protect the ferry established upon the river, and to keep it secure for the troops and supplies to be forwarded by Inspector-General Churchill, commanding the rear column, Captain Fraser was directed to construct a redoubt as a *tête de pont* on the right bank, and, on the left, a field-work ; — to be defended by two companies. A force sufficient to carry into effect such a purpose being detached from the column, the general pushed on to San Juan Bautista. This town contains two thousand inhabitants, all Mexicans. The buildings are of stone, or unburnt bricks (*adobe*), and, with but little preparation, are capable of being easily defended against a superior force. Not the slightest resistance, however, was offered, although the people are represented as being exceedingly hostile toward us. But a few weeks before our arrival, three or four companies of dragoons are said to have been quartered there ; but they had fallen back on the main forces assembled at Monterey. Presidio, like Bexar, Guerrero, &c., was one of the points established early in the settlement of the country for the confinement and labor of state prisoners ; and by an edict of the king of Spain, published in 1772, it was created a military post, and made one of the cordon then formed for the protection of the frontier.

"The Jesuits erected a large mission within a mile of the city similar to the Álamo, La Purísima Concepcion, San José, San Juan, and Espada, near

San Antonio. It is a massive structure, built entirely of stone, but now fast falling to decay. When we passed it, the wind was howling through its ruined arches, like a voice of mourning for those gone from beneath them, never to return. Mitred bishop and cowled monk, veiled nun and timid devotee, have long since passed away; and the grass and wild-flowers grow in the deserted corridors and over the crumbling walls, and flocks of goats herd in the solitary courts.

" The country in the vicinity of this city we found to be very fertile, especially where it was artificially irrigated. Cotton, sugar, corn, wheat, sweet potatoes, and almost every description of garden vegetables, besides figs, oranges, peaches, and other fruits, were raised with but little labor, and in considerable abundance. We were able to procure a sufficient supply of forage for the use of the command, and at very reasonable rates.

" Going from thence westward, the column was obliged to march twenty-six miles without water, when it arrived at the town of San Juan de Nava, situated in the middle of an immense plain, and watered entirely by irrigating ditches, which are said to have their fountains in a range of hills twenty miles to the left of the trace. This town is represented as containing twelve hundred inhabitants, and is built entirely of *adobe*. Three fourths of the houses were not occupied at all, and were fast becoming untenantable. The people, with two or three exceptions, were wretchedly poor, and even more ignorant than the

Indians of our plains. The business of the place is the raising of stock, which is tended by herdsmen, and driven from point to point upon the prairie, that spreads out almost to the horizon on every side. In the immediate vicinity of Nava there are extensive fields of corn; and there, likewise, a sufficient supply was procured for the forage of all the animals of the column.

"From Presidio to Nava, the whole country is a perfect level. In the time of the Jesuits, it was all highly cultivated; but now there is not a single human habitation between those two places. In the olden times, when it was smiling with plentiful crops of corn and grain, and was enlivened by the voices of husbandmen, the lowing of cows, the bleating of numerous flocks, the tinkling of bells, and the noise and hum of life, how beautiful it must have been, compared with its present desolation! Marks of the irrigating dikes traverse the plain in every direction; and at distant intervals, along the wayside, are seen the ruins of many of the ancient granaries, once filled with plentiful harvests, but now empty, and fast crumbling back to the level from whence they were reared.

"A few miles west of Nava, and to the left of General Wool's trace, there is a beautiful island of timber, which the Mexicans call *El Arbolado de los Ángeles*, — The Grove of the Angels. It is said to surround a fine spring of water, and is considered by the inhabitants as a sacred place. This is mentioned merely to illustrate the fact, that in this country, as in all others where the people are ignorant and superstitious, every natural object of beauty or sublimity, — whether mountain, plain, grove, or river, — is invested with some name calculated to awaken poetic and religious associations.

"The next city we visited was San Fernando de Rosas, containing between three and four thousand souls. It is embosomed in an extensive *mot* of timber, which, from its size, and the character of the trees, we supposed must have been planted when the city itself was first built. A fine stream of clear water, called *Arroyo Escondido*, — Hidden Brook, — runs on nearly three sides of it; and, stretching off all around, lies one of the most fertile plains in Mexico. There are two extensive plazas in San Fernando, each surrounded by the residences of the most wealthy citizens, which, although built of stone and in the Mexican style, have an air of neatness and taste we had hardly expected to see. The people we found to be very friendly in their feelings toward us; and whatever supplies we required, they furnished with much cheerfulness. When we commenced our line of march the next day, every eye was turned to take one more look of San Fernando, — literally, *of Roses*. And the scene it presented, with the quaint dome of its old church surmounted by a cross, and rising above the surrounding foliage, — the pure white of its edifices, glistening here and there through the dark green trees, — and its singular position, like that of an oasis, not in a desert, but on an uninhabited plain, — was one of the most picturesque and pleasing we had ever beheld, and one we shall long love to remember.

"Our course now became more southerly, the direction being for the head waters of the Santarita, and a pass through the Sierra de San José. We had not proceeded far before the country began to be more sterile and broken, and long ranges of mountains to skirt the horizon, both upon our right hand and upon our left; while, in front, a formidable chain of them presented a barrier which it appeared impossible we should ever be able to pass with our artillery and immensely long train of wagons. However, as we proceeded, valley after valley opened before us, through which our road wound upwards, until at last we attained their very summit. Even were there room enough in this letter for the execution of such a purpose, it would be impossible to describe the magnificence of the view then spread out before us. Toward the east we looked down on the widely extended plain over which we had so long been journeying. In the distance the grove of San Fernando was still visible; while at our feet the valley of the Santarita lay like a map, with the winding course of the river distinctly traced upon it by the dark line of foliage that fringes its banks. On either hand the peaks of the range upon which we then stood appeared less and less as they became more removed in perspective, until, in the far-off blue, their outlines faded from our sight, and mingled with the faint undulations of the surrounding horizon; while, in the west, the Sierra de

Santa Rosa ascended like a huge and battlemented wall, with its serrated crest jutting aloft in strong relief against the clear sky, and its precipitous sides hung about with festoons of white and purple clouds.

"The San José mountains are clad only with a thin covering of grass, sprinkled here and there with isolated tufts of sotol, cactus, palmetto, and *yucca aloifolia*. Their upper stratum is fossiliferous limestone, but below they are reported as being very rich in silver and copper. Many years ago, a mine is said to have been opened a few miles to the left of our road, and operations in it were carried on with considerable success; but at length the Camanches became so troublesome, that the workmen were obliged to abandon it.

"From these mountains we descended through a tortuous gorge to the Llano de San José, — a broad plain, extending with few interruptions to the foot of the Sierra de Santa Rosa, a distance of thirty miles; and our route lay directly across it. Midway in this plain, and only three miles apart, we encountered two formidable rivers, — the Álamos and Sabinas, which, at their junction, form the Solado, an affluent to the Rio Bravo from the west, and uniting with it at Guerrero. They were each about forty yards in width, upwards of four feet in depth, and had a current of almost incredible rapidity. In short, they were absolute torrents; to cross which we had neither bridges nor boats, nor the means wherewith to construct them; and it was almost a matter of impossibility for horses or mules to maintain their footing in the water, even for a moment. However, by the assistance of ropes and the active exertions of the men, the difficulties they presented were at length overcome; and all the forces, with the cannon, and the ammunition and provision trains, consisting of two hundred heavily laden wagons, passed them both, without any material loss or accident.

"The direction of our march was then for the city of Santa Rosa, which is situated immediately at the foot of the Sierra of that name. It contains between two and three thousand inhabitants, is built of the same material as the other towns we had passed, and is capable of being as easily defended. Many years ago, it was a place of much importance from the rich veins of silver found in its vicinity; but, the political dissensions of this unhappy country prostrating, as they did, every thing like enterprise, the mines, by not being worked, were allowed to become filled with water, from which they have not yet been entirely cleared. It has been left for an American citizen, named Dr. Long, a resident in Santa Rosa, to undertake their drainage; and he will soon, no doubt, reap an abundant reward for his labors.

"The General entered the city with his whole force on the 24th day of October, and without meeting the slightest opposition from the inhabitants. They, in turn, likewise furnished all the supplies he required; and, in fact, regarded the approach of his column with feelings of less dread than they would have done, had it been composed of troops of their own nation. Before the Centre Division left San Antonio de Bexar, General Wool had made every effort to procure accurate information respecting the various routes to Chihuahua. He was assured, that whichever he should select, he must of necessity pass near or through Santa Rosa; and that from there he might have it in his power to make choice of any of the three following, viz. through Nacimiento del Rio, or Head of the River Sabinas, *viâ* San Carlos and Álamo; through Puerto de Obayos, by the way of Cuatro Ciénagas and Santa Catarina; or through Monclova and Parras. The whole country between the Sierra de Santa Rosa and Chihuahua, as far north as Paso del Norte and south to Monclova, was represented as consisting of mountains and extensive arid plains, with few inhabitants and no supplies, and destitute, in a great measure, of water. When he reached Santa Rosa, he found these representations confirmed, and that the two first-named roads were altogether impracticable, for precisely those reasons. To a great extent they were nothing but mule-trails, over which, so far as he could learn, no wagon had ever passed, and where, too, for distances exceeding ninety miles, not one drop of water was to be found. To attempt to lead an army over such a country by such roads would, therefore, have been an act of madness; and one which could not for a moment be seriously thought of. He accordingly adopted the only alternative left him, which was to push on to Monclova, and from thence to Parras, where he would strike the great road from Saltillo to Chihuahua, upon which he could, without much further difficulty, proceed to the latter place. Our course was, therefore, changed directly south, through the valley lying between the Sierras of Santa Rosa and San José. For nearly the whole distance we met with few indications that the country was at all inhabited, save occasional flocks of sheep and goats, tended by solitary *pastores*, and numbering, in some instances, as many as 20,000.

"As we proceeded, the barrenness and sterility of the valley increased; the soil being unable to support much else beside the countless varieties of the cactus, dwarf *mesquite*, *sotol*, *yuca*, and the celebrated *agave Americana*,— the *century plant* of the north, and the *maguey* of Mexico. From the agave the people of this country make their national drink,— *pulque*, the process of manufacturing which has been so often described; and this, when distilled, forms a nauseous and intoxicating liquor, called *mescal*.

"The mountain scenery, surrounding us on every side, we had never seen equalled; and many was the picture presented to us, when the sight of long ranges and groups of them, with their precipitous sides, now in deep shadow, now standing sharply out in the bright sunlight, would have filled with ecstasy a Salvator Rosa.

"At length we arrived at the Paso de las Hermanas, situated in which is an extensive hacienda, occupied by Señor Miguel Blanco, one of the most influential citizens of Coahuila. He received us with much courtesy, and extended towards the officers the hospitalities of his mansion. Going through this pass, we at once entered into the great valley of Monclova, watered by a river of the same name and the Rio Nadadores,— each an affluent to the Solado. Our course then lay in a southerly direction across this valley, till we arrived at the city of Monclova itself, before which General Wool again encamped his column. Where no resistance had been made on the part of the people, no surrender of any city through which he had passed had been demanded by the General; but, as the authorities of this place had made a protest against his advance upon it, he determined at once to take formal possession of the town, and accordingly, on the 3d of November, entered it with all his forces, and had the national flag displayed from the top of the Governor's palace, situated on the principal plaza. Here it was determined at once to establish a dépôt, and to collect all the corn and flour from the surrounding country it would be possible to obtain. This would obviate the necessity of depending on their being received by the long and, in a wet season, totally impracticable route from Port La Vaca, or even from Camargo; to which point a direct communication was immediately opened, it being, for land carriages, 408 miles nearer to Monclova than the former place. The General intended to relinquish all hope of receiving supplies from the east so long as any possibility existed of gathering them up in the country; and every exertion was accordingly made to carry such a purpose into effect. It was ascertained that large quantities of wheat and corn had been sent from Monclova, and the neighboring town Ciénagas, to supply the Mexican army at Monterey, and, more recently, at Saltillo ; and, on the very day we entered the city, 10,000 pounds of flour, which was going in that direction, were seized and at once turned into our dépôt.

" General Taylor having sent orders for the Centre Division not to proceed beyond Monclova until the end of the armistice, or the receipt of other instructions, it was obliged to lie there for the period of twenty-seven days. All this time was occupied in perfecting the discipline of the troops, in the collection of stores, as before stated, and in making extensive reconnoissances of the surrounding country. During that time Inspector-General Churchill came up with the rear column. By his arrival our train was also enlarged by 100 wagons more, well filled with supplies.

" On the 24th of November, — the armistice having expired, — the whole division, with the exception of a command of about 250 men, which was left to guard the dépôt at Monclova, took up its line of march for Parras, 180 miles distant; the general course being nearly south-west. If you will lay before you a Spanish or Mexican map, you will be able to trace our route through the following places, viz. Castaña, Marqués, Bajan, La Joya, Punta de Estañosa, Punta de Reata, Jaral, San Antonio, Teneja, Ciénaga Grande, Galera, and Ojuelos, on to Parras, at which place we arrived on the 5th instant, and are now encamped before the town.

" Parras is said to contain 6000 inhabitants. It is

built in such a manner as to render it more difficult of capture than any town we have yet seen in the Republic. The streets are exceedingly narrow and crooked, and nearly every one of them has on each side a thick *adobe* wall, some ten or twelve feet in height. A high range of mountains rises up immediately in the rear of the city, easy to be maintained; while along its entire front, and skirting each of its flanks, are immense vineyards, surrounded, also, by walls of great height and thickness. Its situation is at the foot of the celebrated Bolson de Malpamí, and is about 100 miles from Saltillo, 200 from Durango, 300 from San Luis de Potosí, 150 from Monterey, and 450 from Chihuahua. It is represented as being near the centre of the best grain-growing region in Mexico; the business of the place, however, is the culture of the grape, and large quantities of wine and brandy, of a superior quality, are annually transported on the backs of mules to all the principal towns throughout the country.

"This city being the key to Chihuahua, General Wool was anxious to reach it much earlier than he did, and would have done so by nearly a month, had it not been for the armistice, as has already been shown. Once being here, he would be at liberty to go with his whole force to that place, or send a detachment to take possession of it, while the rest would be free to coöperate with the Army of Occupation, or to move on Durango or Zacatecas, as the exigencies of the service should most require. As it was, however, intelligence was received, previous to his arrival here, that most of the troops, which had assembled in the upper provinces, had fallen back upon the lower, thereby rendering the necessity of the whole division marching in that direction out of the question. And now the proximity of Santa Anna, and the great efforts he is making to concentrate and prepare for the field the most formidable army Mexico has ever arrayed against us, imperiously demand that we remain at or near the position we at present occupy, that we may be ready at any moment to form a junction with General Taylor, and perform our part in the most fearful game that has been played for many a year, and one in which we have Santa Anna for an antagonist; — but who yet has been able to compute the stakes?

"I have already made this letter too long; but, before I close it, permit me to say, that, for the maintenance of this column, almost every article, whether of ammunition, subsistence, or other stores, had to be transported from La Vaca here, — a distance of 800 miles. The labor required to procure the necessary wagons, teams, &c., and to organize them into trains, though great in itself, was not to be considered in comparison with that of guarding them through a hostile and, in a measure, unknown country, and bringing them, without loss, over desolate plains, rapid and almost impassable rivers, over high sierras, and through dangerous defiles, where it was incumbent upon every man not only to exercise the utmost vigilance, but literally to put his shoulder to the wheel. Wherever we went, the necessities of our position urgently demanded that we should be encumbered with all these things so indispensable to our existence, to the success of our enterprise, and to what, in any situation, would make us an effective force, in despite of the naturally inhospitable barrenness of the country, or the efforts of an active enemy in laying it waste before us. As yet our progress has not been retarded by the firing of a single shot; but our officers and men have labored with a zeal and fidelity, which can never be appreciated but by those who have witnessed their efforts, and observed from day to day how many have been the obstacles they have overcome to reach this advanced position. The continued evidences of their energy and perseverance have been sufficient, aside from the other and more weighty considerations of patriotism and desire for distinction, to warrant the belief that the flag of our far-off and beloved country is safe when intrusted to such hands. C."

Four days after the above letter was written, the Centre Division left Parras for Agua Nueva.

See Appendix, B.

B.
(See page 5.)

After the Battle of Buena Vista had been fought, several officers are said to have claimed the honor of having chosen the ground upon which it took place. As the selection of the field had been made by General Wool himself, he desired to correct the mistake which those officers were laboring under, evidently from ignorance of that fact. Accordingly he wrote the following note to Captain Carleton, of the 1st Dragoons, who, as one of his aides-de-camp, was with him at the time the choice was made.

"Buena Vista, July 27, 1847.

"SIR: You may recollect, that the next evening (that of the 22d December last) after my arrival at Agua Nueva from Parras, I left my camp to visit Generals Butler and Worth, who were both reported as being confined by illness at Saltillo. I was accompanied by Captains Lee, Hughes, Chapman, my aide, and yourself, acting aide-de-camp. Before we reached La Encantada, it became quite dark; and, whilst passing through the valley toward Saltillo, some of the party, on several occasions, had to dismount in order to keep the road. It was too dark, owing to a fog, to make a reconnoissance of the valley * that night.

"The next morning, I returned to Agua Nueva, accompanied only by yourself. The remainder of my staff did not leave Saltillo until toward night. When I arrived at the Pass, or Narrows, where Washington's Battery was stationed during the Battle of Buena Vista, I halted to examine the position. Will you do me the favor to state what passed, or was said, on that

---

* Viz. the Pass of Buena Vista.

occasion, in reference to the Pass, the surrounding heights, and the gullies on the right of the position?

"I am, very respectfully,
"Your obedient servant,
"JOHN E. WOOL, *U. S. A.*
"To Captain J. H. CARLETON,
"*1st Dragoons, Present.*"

To this letter Captain Carleton replied as follows:

"Buena Vista, Mexico, July 27, 1847.

"GENERAL: I have been honored with the receipt of your note of this date, and, in reply, would state, that, by a reference to my '*Journal of the Marches, &c., of General Wool's Column*,' I find, that, on the 21st of December, 1846, you arrived in the valley of La Encantada, with your whole force, consisting of cavalry, artillery, and infantry, with their complete trains, and encamped at Agua Nueva, situated at its southern termination. That point is twenty miles in advance of Saltillo, which city was then occupied by General Worth, to whose assistance you had marched from Parras, a distance of one hundred and fifteen miles, in less than four days. At that time, the command of General Worth was only a brigade, and he had sent, by express, a request to you, at Parras, to join him with your column, as soon as possible, to assist in repelling an attack, then daily expected from the enemy in force under General Santa Anna.

"About the same time, General Butler arrived at Saltillo from Monterey. On the evening of the 22d of December, you left your camp, at Agua Nueva, to visit both him and General Worth,— it being reported that they were confined to their beds in consequence of the wounds they had received. You were accompanied by Captains Lee, Hughes, and Chapman, U. S. A., by your aide, Lieutenant McDowell, and by myself, then on duty also as one of your aides. It was quite dark when you left Agua Nueva; and, when you arrived at that part of the Pass of Buena Vista known as La Angostura, a heavy fog, accompanied by rain, had set in, rendering it so much more so, that it was with the utmost difficulty the road could be kept. Indeed, the officers who were with you were frequently obliged to dismount and seek for it on either hand. It was past eleven o'clock at night when you and your party reached Saltillo. The next day, when your interview with Generals Butler and Worth was concluded, you started on your return to your camp at Agua Nueva, accompanied only by myself, all the other officers who had gone to Saltillo with you being still detained there by official business. When you had proceeded as far as La Angostura, one mile in advance of the hacienda of San Juan de la Buena Vista, you halted, and, after having glanced over the ground on each side, you said to me; 'Mr. Carleton, this is the very spot of all others I have yet seen in Mexico, which I should select for battle, were I obliged with a small army to fight a large one.'

"You then pointed out to me what you conceived to be the great military advantages it possessed, and said that the net-work of deeply-worn channels on the right would completely protect that flank; that the heights, on your left, would command the road, while the ravines in front of them, and which extend back to the mountain on that side, would cripple the movements of the enemy, should he attempt to turn that flank. You continued conversing with me on this subject, until, as you may recollect, we met Lieutenant McCown, 4th Artillery, a mile or more farther on. So forcibly was I impressed with your choice, and all you had said in favor of it, that, immediately after my arrival at Agua Nueva, I described the place to some of the officers of your staff,—I think to Inspector-General Churchill, and his assistant, Captain Drum, U. S. A., saying at the time, that you had selected it for a battle-ground, and repeating all you had stated in relation to it.

"It may not be improper likewise to add, that, on the 26th of December, General Butler visited you at Agua Nueva, and that, on the 27th, before he returned to Saltillo, he gave you an order to move with your troops, and select, in the neighborhood of La Encantada, or farther down the stream towards Saltillo, a suitable place, and there encamp. As this order was entirely discretionary as to the precise locality for your proposed camp, you chose the plain between La Angostura and the hacienda, before alluded to, as the best, because it was not only less exposed to the bleak winds, which continually swept through the Pass at La Encantada, and which, at that season of the year, would cause the troops much suffering, as we were all in tents and fuel was very scarce, but offered the additional advantage of an abundant supply of pure water; and, besides, was just in the rear of what you had selected as a strong point of defence.

"That evening (the 28th), General Butler sent you an order to return to La Encantada, and encamp there. You wrote a note to him, requesting, for reasons which you assigned, that he would permit you to remain where you were, and sent it by Colonel Hardin. Captain Drum and myself accompanied Colonel Hardin, and were present at the interview between General Butler and him. During the conversation that ensued after your note had been delivered, Colonel Hardin, among other reasons which he gave why he hoped your request might be complied with, urged the fact that you were near a point which you believed you could maintain, in case the enemy advanced upon you from the direction of San Luis de Potosí. General Butler said he would not revoke his order, and remarked, that, if the Mexican army came, he had already chosen a ground for battle, and even gone so far as to fix the points to be occupied by the several corps. That ground was the broad plain immediately in front of Saltillo; and I think he also said he had already prepared roads for the artillery, leading from the city up to it. I have mentioned all these circumstances, to show with what anxiety and exertion you endeavored to be permitted to occupy a point within striking distance of the one you had selected as the best for battle. On the 30th of December, your whole command was obliged to retrace its steps to La

Encantada, which it did with evident reluctance, as all the officers agreed entirely with you in opinion as to the disadvantages arising from such a change of position.

"Previous to the time when you first went to Saltillo (the 22d), not one of your officers had ever gone through the Pass of Buena Vista. All those who went with you, on that occasion, were prevented, as I have shown, by the extreme darkness, even from seeing the great road on which they sought to travel, and could not, therefore, have had at that time a favorable opportunity for making military reconnoissances. You returned from the city, and had pointed out the position to me, as I have stated, before they repassed over it. The choice and partialities of the officers in Saltillo, it is fair to presume, for many reasons, were coincident with those expressed by General Butler. When General Taylor came up from Monterey, he saw, at a glance, that your views were correct; and, although he moved the whole army forward to Agua Nueva, as there he could have an extensive plain for the drill and discipline of the troops, with wood and water convenient, and besides, by doing so, could take the initiatory step in one of the most beautiful pieces of strategy of modern times,— still, when, by the advance of Santa Anna, the moment had arrived to gain the grand result by feigning a precipitate retreat, that retreat was but a rapid movement back to the identical spot which you had chosen, and to which the Mexican army was hurriedly drawn on, with all its fatigue and disarray, consequent

APPENDIX. 183

upon a forced march of upwards of forty miles; and here, on the 22d and 23d of February, 1847, was fought the battle of Buena Vista. The result of that conflict afforded conclusive evidence of the correctness of your first remark; — for there four thousand six hundred and ten Americans contended successfully against upwards of twenty-two thousand Mexicans.

"This letter, General, is but a dry detail of facts; but I hope they are set forth with sufficient clearness to prevent their being misunderstood.

"I have the honor to be, very respectfully,
"Your obedient servant,
"JAMES HENRY CARLETON,
"*Captain U. S. 1st Dragoons.*
"To Brigadier-General JOHN E. WOOL,
"*Commanding, &c. &c. &c., Present.*"

The following is the note which General Wool wrote, acknowledging the receipt of the foregoing letter:

"Head-Quarters, Buena Vista, Mexico,
August 1, 1847.

"MY DEAR SIR: I give you many thanks for your interesting letter, of the 27th ultimo, relating to the selection of the field of battle, to meet General Santa Anna and his forces, called by him La Angostura, and where, he said, on the two eventful days of the 22d and 23d of February last, 'blood flowed in torrents, and the field of battle was strewed with the bodies of the dead.'

"The great credit given, throughout the United States, to officers said to have suggested the field of battle to me, induced me to call your attention to the subject. Your letter, which is strictly in accordance with my own recollections, settles the question. I never thought, however, that any great credit was due on account of the selection, for it appeared to me too obvious to escape observation; still, if great credit is due to any one, it belongs to myself, for, in company with you, on the morning of the 23d of December last, it attracted my attention, as set forth in your letter, and before any person had indicated to me the position.

"I am very truly yours,
JOHN E. WOOL, *U. S. A.*

"To Captain JAMES H. CARLETON,
"*1st Dragoons, Present.*"

General Wool permitted the reporter of the New Orleans "Picayune" to make a copy of Captain Carleton's letter for that paper. After it was published, it became the occasion of several communications, published in various newspapers, by different officers. But, as none of these communications controverted the facts it specified, they remained unanswered. Captain George W. Hughes, of the Topographical Engineers, was one of the officers who had claimed to have suggested to General Wool the battle-ground, and to have pointed out its advantages while in the discharge of his official duties. As soon as Captain Carleton's letter was published, he addressed a long communication to the Editors of the "National Intelligencer," in which he says; "General Wool (on the *twenty-seventh* of December) instructed me to select a camp [!], in reference to a *field of battle*, at some point between Encantada and Saltillo, — not, however, to approach nearer than three miles of the latter place. I do, however, most solemnly aver, that the General gave me no other instructions than those above mentioned, and that he never once named to me, nor even hinted at, Buena Vista, — nor did any other person." "As a mere encampment, the place chosen by me, at Buena Vista, was unexceptionable. It was on a smooth, beautiful plain, well sheltered from the prevailing winds, with cool, delicious water in front and rear, good grazing in the vicinity, and plenty of fuel hard by. Important as were all these considerations, they were not the most important. Its highest recommendation was its remarkably defensible character. As a comfortable, agreeable, and convenient camp, it was not necessary to look farther."

"No one but myself, I believe, ever committed himself, in writing at least, or in any other way (unless, perhaps, by some slight, trivial phrase), by suggesting Buena Vista as a battle-ground, until after the battle was fought. Its advantage then became apparent, no doubt, to hundreds! I regret that there should have been any controversy about this matter; and I certainly should have taken no part in it, but for the fact that my memoir was published during my absence with the army; and that this publication has been made necessary by an attempt to deprive me of the credit of some little service which my friends think I have rendered to the country."

For the information of the reader, it is necessary to state, that Captain Hughes left Saltillo for Brazos Santiago early in January, nearly six weeks before the battle was fought. He has not been upon the ground since. All he states in reference to the selection of the camp at *Buena Vista* is probably correct. If there is any thing in Captain Carleton's letter calculated to "deprive" Captain Hughes "of the credit of some little service, which his friends think he has rendered to the country" by that important act, it is there through mistake, and is hereby recalled. No one could wish to deprive the gallant captain of his hard-earned honors. It is granted that he did select that encampment, as he claims to have done. In return, will not that chivalrous officer extend the same generosity toward General Wool? If Captain Hughes imagines, for a moment, that General Wool desires to receive credit for having chosen " the encampment at Buena Vista," he does the General great injustice. But why should there be any controversy at all? General Wool claims to have selected the battle-ground at *La Angostura*,—Captain Hughes claims to have selected the site of an encampment at *Buena Vista*. THE TWO PLACES ARE ONE MILE AND A HALF APART.

APPENDIX. 187

C.
(See page 37.)

Ejército Libertador Republicano,
General en Gefe, Señoría de Campaña.

Está V. S. rodeado de veinte mil hombres, y humanamente [no] puede escapar de sufrir una derrota y de ser anichilado con los suyos; pero mereciendome V. S. consideracion y particular aprecio, quiero evitarle una catástrofe, y al efecto le hago esta intimacion para que se rinda á discrecion, seguro de que sea tratado con la consideracion propia del carácter Mejicano; concediendole al efecto una hora de término, que correrá desde el momento en que se presente un parlamentario en el campo de V. S.

Con este motivo protesto á V. S. mi atenta consideracion.

Dios y Libertad! Campo en la Encantada, Febrero 22, 1847.

ANTO. LOPEZ DE SANTA ANNA.

Señor Gen. Z. TAYLOR,
Com'dte de las Fuerzas de los E. U.

D.
(See page 82.)

Boston, June 26, 1848.

MY DEAR COLONEL: I have recently written a History of the Battle of Buena Vista, in which I have spoken of the important and highly distinguished service you rendered during the darkest period of that sanguinary conflict, in rallying the troops belonging to the Second Regiment of Indiana Volunteers, which had given way before a vastly superior force of the enemy, and were flying the field. Will you do me the favor to state how many, in your opinion, you rallied on the occasion to which I have alluded?

I have the honor to be,
Very faithfully, yours,
JAMES HENRY CARLETON,
Captain U. S. 1st Dragoons.

To ROGER SHERMAN DIX,
Brevet Lieut.-Col. U. S. A., Present.

Boston, June 27, 1848.

MY DEAR CAPTAIN: I have received your letter of yesterday, informing me that you have written a History of the Battle of Buena Vista, and inquiring how many of the 2d Indiana Volunteers were rallied after that regiment had " given way before a vastly superior force of the enemy, and were flying the field."

I am glad to learn, that one who had the best possible opportunity of observing the battle, and who distinguished himself by some of its most brilliant acts, has undertaken to write its history.

In reply to your inquiry, I would state, that nearly 200 of the Indiana Regiment, about *two thirds* of those who had broken and fallen back, were rallied, and returned to the field.

You have, without doubt, (as I am sure it is your intention to do to all) done full justice to our gallant

APPENDIX.

friend, Brevet Major T. B. Linnard, for the valuable assistance he rendered on the occasion referred to.

Thanking you for the very complimentary expressions contained in your letter,

I remain, my dear Captain,

Most faithfully yours,

R. S. DIX,
Brevet Lieut.-Col. U. S. A.

Captain J. H. CARLETON,
 1st U. S. Dragoons, Present.

E.

(See page 128.)

Return of the Killed, Wounded, and Missing, of the Army of Occupation, at Buena Vista, Mexico, Feb. 22d, 23d, 1847.

Corps	Killed — Colonels	Lieutenant Colonels	Adjutants	Captains	Subalterns	Non-com'd Officers, Musicians, Artificers, and Privates	Commiss'd Officers	Aggregate	Wounded — Brigadier-Generals	Colonels	Majors	Captains	Subalterns	Non-com'd Officers, Musicians, Artificers, and Privates	Commiss'd Officers	Aggregate	Mis'g — Non-com'd Officers, Musicians, Artificers, and Privates	Commiss'd Officers	Aggregate	Total — Commiss'd Officers	Non-com'd Officers, Musicians, Artificers, and Privates	Aggregate
General Staff,............							1	1	1						3	3				4		4
First Dragoons,............																				1	6	7
Second Dragoons,............						1		1					1		1	7		2	2	1	24	25
Third Artillery,............						5		5				1	1	21	2	22		2	2	1	25	26
Fourth Artillery,............					2	38	2	40				1	1	20	5	56				7	91	98
Mississippi Riflemen,............						26	1	27					5	51	5	34				6	55	61
Kentucky Cavalry,............		1		1		15	2	17					1	29	3	32		2	2	5	50	53
Arkansas Cavalry,............		1		1		41	3	44				1	3	3	32			4		7	96	103
Second Kentucky Foot,............	1		1			26	3	29		1			2	54	3	57				6	42	47
First Illinois Foot,............	1			1	1	38	10	48		1	1		4	16	2	18		3	4	16	110	126
Second Illinois Foot,............	1				1	29	3	32					2	69	6	75		4		11	96	107
Second Indiana Foot,............				2		8		9					4	63	8	71				4	61	65
Third Indiana Foot,............						12		14					6	53	3	56		7	7	3	20	23
Company of Texas Volunt'rs,............															1	2						
Grand aggregate,............	3	1	1	8	15	229	28	267	1	1	1	11	28	415	41	456		23	23	69	677	746

Note. — The above was based upon reports sent in soon after the battle. The following Return by Inspector-General Sylvester Churchill, being carefully compiled from the Muster Rolls of February 26th, 1847, is considered more correct in every particular, owing to the difference of date, and the time that had elapsed in which to detect any errors that might inadvertently have crept into the original reports.

HEAD-QUARTERS ARMY OF OCCUPATION,
Agua Nueva, Mexico, March 6, 1847.

Z. TAYLOR,
Major-General U. S. Army commanding.

W. W. S. BLISS, A. A. G.

APPENDIX. 191

REPORT OF THE KILLED, WOUNDED, AND MISSING, IN THE BATTLE OF BUENA VISTA,

February 22d and 23d, 1847, by Detachments, Regiments, &c., as shown mostly by the Muster Rolls of February 28, 1847.

BUENA VISTA, MEXICO. S. CHURCHILL,
April, 1847. *Inspector-General.*

REGULARS.

GENERAL STAFF.

ADJUTANT-GENERAL'S DEPARTMENT.

Killed.			Wounded.		Missing.	Killed, wounded, and miss'g.	Total.
Names.	Rank.	No.	Rank.	No.			
Capt. Geo. Lincoln,	A. A. G.	1	....	...	...	1	1

CORPS OF ENGINEERS.

			1st Lt.,	1	...	1	2

THIRD REGIMENT OF ARTILLERY.
CAPT. SHERMAN'S COMPANY E.

			2d. Lt.	1			
			Privates,	14			
			Total, ..	15		15	17

* This report shows the number to be *eighty* less than was exhibited in that of the Assistant Adjutant-General, made a day or two after the battle, the excess in which may be accounted for by the confusion in camp at the time, and its embracing the *slightly* wounded, many of whom, and of those reported "*missing*," were "present for duty" at the subsequent muster.   S. C.

Captain Bragg's Company C.

Killed.			Wounded.		Missing.	Killed, wounded, and miss'g.	Total.
Names.	Rank.	No.	Rank.	No.			
Christ. F. Waibinger,	Private,	1	Corp., .. Privates,	1 3			
			Total, ..	4		5	22

FOURTH REGIMENT OF ARTILLERY.
Captain Washington's Company B.

Killed			Wounded		Missing	K/W/M	Total
Calvin Doughty,	Private,	1					
Edwin Holley,	"	2	1st. Lt.,	1			
Henry Kinks,	"	3	2d. Lt.,	1			
Thomas Weekly,	"	4	Sergts.,	2			
Kausler Puffer,	"	5	Privates,	18			
John Green,	"	6					
	Total, ..	6	Total, ..	22	..	28	50

FIRST REGIMENT OF DRAGOONS.
Company A.

			Privates,	3	..	3	53

Company E.

			Capt., ...	1			
			2d Lieut.,	1			
			Farrier, .	1			
			Privates,	3			
			Total,...	6	..	6	59
Total in 1st Dragoons,	......	...	....	9	..	..	..

Captain L. B. Webster's Company of 1st Artillery, garrisoned the redoubt at Saltillo.

APPENDIX. 193

SECOND REGIMENT OF DRAGOONS.
COMPANY E.

KILLED.			WOUNDED.		Missing.	Killed, wounded, and miss'g.	Total.
Names.	Rank.	No.	Rank.	No.			
			B.Lt.Col.	1	..	2	61
			Private,	1			

VOLUNTEERS.

GENERALS AND GENERAL STAFF.

			Bgr. Gen.	1	..	1	62

ARKANSAS MOUNTED REGIMENT.
FIELD AND STAFF.

Archibald Yell, ...	Col....	1	......	..	..	1	63

CAPTAIN TAYLOR'S COMPANY A.

George Norwood,....	Private,	1	Sergt., ..	1			
Andrew Teague, ...	"	2	Corp., ..	1			
			Privates,	4			
	Total, ..	2	......	6	..	8	71

CAPTAIN DANLEY'S COMPANY B.

John B. Pelham, Jr.,	Private,	1					
Thomas G. Rowland,	"	2	Privates,	2			
	Total, ..	2	......	2	..	4	75

CAPTAIN PATRICK'S COMPANY C.

David Hogan,......	Private,	1					
———— Williams,....	"	2	Privates,	3			
	Total, ..	2	......	3	..	5	80

Captain Porter's Company **D.**

Killed.			Wounded.		Missing.	Killed, wounded, and miss'g.	Total.
Names.	Rank	No.	Rank.	No.			
Andrew R. Porter,..	Captain,	1					
Richard M. Saunders,	Corp., ..	1					
Green H. Higgins,..	Private,	1					
Harrison Penter,....	"	2	Sergt., ..	1			
William Phipps,....	"	3	Privates,	3			
	Total,..	5	......	4	..	9	89

Captain Dillard's Company **F.**

Darian Steward, ...	Corp., ..	1	Sergt., ..	1			
Harman Winn, ...	Private,	1	Privates,	2			
	Total, ..	2	......	3	..	5	94

Captain Hunter's Company **G.**

			Private, .	1	1*	2	96

Captain W. H. Preston's Company **H.**

Wilson W. Tomberlin,	Corp., ..	1					
George Martin,......	Private,	1	Private,.	1			
	Total, ..	2	......	1	..	3	99

Captain Inglish's Company **I.**

Jacob Ray,.........	Private,	1	1st Lt...	1			
William Robinson,..	"	2	Privates,	2			
	Total,..	2	......	3		5	104
Total in Arkansas Mounted Reg.	....	18	......	23	1	42	

* Private.
Companies E, (Pike's,) and K, (Preston's,) stationed in Saltillo, six miles from the field of battle, on the 22d, and with May's squadron on the field, on the 23d.

APPENDIX.

KENTUCKY MOUNTED REGIMENT.
Field and Staff.

Killed.			Wounded.		Missing.	Killed, wounded, and miss'g.	Total.
Names.	Rank.	No.	Rank.	No.			
Edward M. Vaughn,	1st Lt. and Adj.	1	……..	..	..	1	105

Captain Wilam's Company C.

J. F. Ellingwood,	Private,	1					
James Leston,	"	2					
John Sanders,	"	3	Privates,	2			
	Total...	3	……	2	..	5	110

Captain Price's Company A.

John D. Miller,	Private,	1	2d Lt., ..	1			
Bronson Warren,	"	2	Privates,	3			
	Total, ..	2	……	4	..	6	116

Captain Clay's Company I.

			2d Lt.,..	1			
			Corp.,…	1			
			Total, ..	2	..	2	118

Captain Beard's Company K.

William W. Bayles,	Corp., ..	1					
Henry Carty,	Private,	1					
Alex. G. Morgan,	"	2					
Nathaniel Ramsey,	"	3					
William Thwaits,	"	4					
Clement Jones,	"	5	Private,	1			
	Total, ..	6	……	1	..	7	125

Captain Heady's Company E.

Killed.			Wounded.		Missing.	Killed, Wounded, and miss'g.	Total.
Names.	Rank.	No.	Rank.	No.			
C. B. Thompson,....	Private,	1	2d Lt., .	1			
			Sergt., .	1			
	Total,..	1	....	2	..	3	128

Captain Pennington's Company G.

Henry Danforth,....	Private,	1					
John Ross,..........	"	2					
J. M. Rowlin, ...	"	3					
Jesse Martin,.......	"	4					
G. F. Lilley,........	"	5					
G. Routson,........	"	6	Priv'ts,	4			
	"						
	Total,..	6	....	4	..	10	138

Captain Shawhan's Company D.

John A. Jones,.....	Private,	1					
Wm. A. M'Clintock,	"	2					
James Pomeroy,....	"	3	Capt.,..	1			
David R. Rodgers,..	"	4	Priv'ts,	6			
	Total, ..	4	....	7	..	11	149

Captain Lillard's Company B.

David J. Lillard,....	Sergt., .	1					
A. J. Martin, ...	Private,	1					
Lewis Sanders,.....	"	2					
Patrick Quigley,....	"	3					
Michael Nouse,.....	"	4					
	Total,..	5				5	154
Total in Kentucky Mounted Reg't,..	....	28	....	22	..	50	

SECOND KENTUCKY FOOT REGIMENT.
Field and Staff.

Killed.			Wounded.		Missing.	Killed, wounded, and miss'g.	Total.
Names.	Rank.	No.	Rank.	No.			
Wm. R. M'Kee, ...	Colonel,	1					
Henry Clay, Jr., ...	Lt. Col.,	1					
	Total,..	2	....	..	..	2	156

Captain Moss's Company A.

Killed.			Wounded.		Missing.	Killed, wounded, and miss'g.	Total.
A. M. Chandoin,....	Private,	1	2d Lt.,.	1			
John W. Smith, ...	"	2	Priv'ts,	2			
	Total,	2	....	3	..	5	161

Captain Chambers's Company B.

Killed.			Wounded.		Missing.	Killed, wounded, and miss'g.	Total.
Henry Wolff,.......	Sergt., .	1					
Wm. Blackwell, ...	Private,	1					
L. B. Bartlett, ...	"	2					
Mager Updyke,.....	"	3	Priv'ts,	3			
	Total, .	4	....	3	..	7	168

Captain Thompson's Company C.

Killed.			Wounded.		Missing.	Killed, wounded, and miss'g.	Total.
Sidney W. Williams,	Corp., ..	1					
Robert M. Baker,...	Private,	1	2d Lt.,.	1			
Micajah Booth,.....	"	2	Sergt., .	1			
William Banks,.....	"	3	Corp.,..	1			
John Moffit,........	"	4	Priv'ts,	3			
	Total, ..	5	....	6	..	11	179

Captain Fry's Company **D.**

Killed.			Wounded.		Missing.	Killed, wounded, and miss'g.	Total.
Names.	Rank.	No.	Rank.	No.			
Peter Trough, ...	Corp.,...	1					
William Hammond,.	Private,	1					
Harvey Jones,......	"	2					
Joseph Walder,.....	"	3	Private,	3			
	Total,	4	....	3	..	7	186

Captain Cutter's Company **E.**

Quincy J. Carlin,...	Sergt., .	1					
Mart. L. Roderburgh,	Musi'n,	1					
Hiram Frazier,......	Private,	1					
John Hearkins,......	"	2					
Robert M'Curdy,....	"	3	Corp., .	1			
Hercules Snow,.....	"	4	Priv'ts,	6			
	Total,	6	....	7	..	13	199

Captain Willis's Company **F.**

Wm. S. Willis, ...	Capt.,..	1					
Harvey Trotter, ...	Private,	1					
	Total,	2	....	..	..	2	201

Captain Dougherty's Company **G.**

James R. Ballard, ..	Private,	1					
John A. Gregory, ...	"	2					
Willis West, ...	"	3	2d Lt.,	1			
Jesse J. Walker,....	"	4	Priv'ts,	3			
	Total, ..	4	....	4	..	8	209

Captain Joyner's Company H.

Killed.			Wounded.		Missing.	Killed, wounded, and miss'g.	Total.
Names.	Rank.	No.	Rank.	No.			
Joseph King,	Sergt.,	1					
John M. Dunlop,	"	2					
William Gilbert,	Private,	1	Sergt.,	1			
William Rham,	"	2	Corp.,	2			
John Williams,	"	3	Priv'ts,	5			
Total,		5	....	8	..	13	222

Captain Turpin's Company I.

Henry Edwards,	Corp.,	1					
Abraham Goodparter,	Private,	1					
John Thorson,	"	2	Priv'ts,	2			
Total,		3	....	2	..	5	227

Captain M. Brayer's Company K.

William Boras,	Private,	1					
David Davis,	"	2					
James Johnson,	"	3					
James Layton,	"	4					
Wm. P. Reynolds,	"	5					
Arthur Thacker,	"	6	Sergt.,	1			
John W. Watson,	"	7	Priv'ts,	6			
Total,		7	....	7	..	14	241
Total in Kentucky Foot Regiment,	....	44	....	43	..	87	

FIRST ILLINOIS REGIMENT.
Field and Staff.

John J. Hardin,	Colonel,	1					
Austin W. Fay,	Mus'n.,	1					
Total,		2	....	..	..	2	243

APPENDIX.

CAPTAIN SMITH'S COMPANY B.

KILLED.			WOUNDED.		Missing.	Killed, wounded, and miss'g.	Total.
Names.	Rank.	No.	Rank.	No.			
F. S. Carter,........	Private,	1	Captain,	1			
			Corp.,...	1			
			Priv'ts,	3			
	Total, ..	1	....	5	..	6	249

CAPTAIN FRY'S COMPANY C.

Merritt Hudson,....	Mus'n.,	1	..	..	..	1	250

CAPTAIN ZABRISKIE'S COMPANY D.

Jacob W. Zabriskie,.	Captain,	1					
Augustus Canaught,	Private,	1	Sergt.,	1			
John Emerson, ...	"	2	Priv'ts,	2			
	Total, ..	3	....	3	..	6	256

CAPTAIN RICHARDSON'S COMPANY E.

Silas Bedell,........	Private,	1					
Henry H. Clark,....	"	2					
Wm. Goodwin, ...	"	3					
James J. Kinman, ..	"	4					
Randolph R. Martin,	"	5					
G. S. Richardson,...	"	6					
Sam'l W. Thompson,	"	7					
Charles Walker, ...	"	8	Priv'ts,	2			
	Total, ..	8	....	2	..	10	266

Companies A, (Morgan's,) and I, (Prentiss's,) stationed in Saltillo.

APPENDIX. 201

Captain Montgomery's Company H.

Killed.			Wounded.		Missing.	Killed, wounded, and miss'g.	Total.
Names.	Rank.	No.	Rank.	No.			
Bryan R. Houghton,	1st Lt.,	1					
William Smith, ...	Mus'n.,	1					
Matthew Dawdy, ...	Private,	1					
Thomas J. Gilbert, ..	"	2					
Elisha C. Mays, ...	"	3	2d Lt.,	1			
John White, ...	"	4	Priv'ts,	3			
	Total, ..	6	....	4	..	10	276

Captain Mower's Company K.

Conrad Burch, ...	Private,	1					
John B. Backman, ..	"	2					
Inglehot Claibsottle,	"	3					
John Gable, ...	"	4					
Aaron Kiersted, ...	"	5					
George Pitson, ...	"	6					
Joseph Shute, ...	"	7					
Wm. Vinkleharker, .	"	8	Priv'ts,	2			
	Total, ..	8	....	2	..	10	286
Total in First Illinois Regiment, ...		29		16	..	45	

SECOND ILLINOIS REGIMENT.

Field and Staff.

			1st Lt. & Adj.	1			
			Sergt. Maj.	1			
			Qr. M. Sergt.	1			
			Total,	3	..	3	289

Captain Coffey's Company A.

Killed.			Wounded.		Missing	Killed, wounded, and miss'g.	Total.
Names.	Rank.	No.	Rank.	No.			
Allen B. Rountree,	2d Lt.,	1	Capt.,	1			
William R. Kinyon,	Private,	1	Sergt.,	1			
Wm. L. Smith,	"	2	Priv'ts,	10			
	Total,	3	....	12	..	15	304

Captain Woodward's Company B.

Killed.			Wounded.		Missing	Killed, wounded, and miss'g.	Total.
Wm. C. Woodward,	Capt.,	1					
John Bartleson,	1st Lt..	1					
Aaron Atherton,	2d Lt...	1					
William Price,	"	2					
Wm. J. Ferguson,	Sergt.,	1					
Joseph W. Emerson,	Private,	1					
George W. Crippen,	"	2					
Abner Durock,	"	3					
John W. Kiger,	"	4					
Richard E. Scott,	"	5	Private,	1			
	Total,	10	....	1	..	11	315

Captain Baker's Company C.

Killed.			Wounded.		Missing	Killed, wounded, and miss'g.	Total.
Edward F. Fletcher,	1st Lt.,	1					
Rodney Ferguson,	2d Lt.,	1					
L. Robbins,	"	2					
William Hibbs,	Corp.,	1	Capt.,	1			
James S. Patten,	Private,	1	2d Lt.,	1			
Amos Woodling,	"	2	Priv.,	11			
	Total,	6	....	13	..	19	334

Companies D, (Wheeler's,) and F, (Hacker's,) stationed at Saltillo.

APPENDIX. 203

Captain Lott's Company E.

Killed.			Wounded.		Missing.	Killed, wounded, and miss'g.	Total.
Names.	Rank.	No.	Rank.	No.			
Timothy Kelley,	2d Lt.,	1					
John Gable,	Private,	1					
Thos. D. O'Connor,	"	2	Priv'ts,	4			
	Total,	3	....	4	..	7	341

Captain Lemon's Company G.

Killed.			Wounded.		Missing.	Killed, wounded, and miss'g.	Total.
Thomas Jenkins,	Private,	1					
David A. Hill,	"	2					
Wm. S. Messinger,	"	3	Priv'ts,	2			
	Total,	3	....	2	..	5	346

Captain Kaith's Company H.

Killed.			Wounded.		Missing.	Killed, wounded, and miss'g.	Total.
Alexander Conze,	Private,	1					
Christian Crossman,	"	2					
George Lartz,	"	3					
Emanuel Schoolcraft,	"	4	2d Lt.,	1			
Franz Weber,	"	5	Priv'ts,	10			
	Total,	5	....	11	2*	18	364

Captain Miller's Company I.

Killed.			Wounded.		Missing.	Killed, wounded, and miss'g.	Total.
Emanuel Bradley,	Private,	1					
Goforth Clark,	"	2					
Henry Cook,	"	3					
John M. Davis,	"	4					
William Hogan,	"	5					
John Lear,	"	6	Sergt.,	1			
John M'Crury,	"	7	Priv'ts,	13			
	Total,	7	....	14	..	21	385

* Privates.

CAPTAIN STARBUCK'S COMPANY K.

KILLED.			WOUNDED.		Missing.	Killed, wounded, and miss'g.	Total.
Names.	Rank.	No.	Rank.	No.			
James C. Steele,....	2d Lt., .	1					
Robert Abernathy,..	Private,	1					
John F. Bowen, ...	"	2					
Wm. S. Jones,......	"	3					
Wm. M. Jones,......	"	4					
John B. Kimzey,....	"	5					
Robert Marlow,.....	"	6					
S. C. Marlow, ...	"	7					
Wm. A. Ragland, ..	"	8					
John B. Wilks,.....	"	9	Priv'ts,	6			
	Total,..	10	....	6		16	401

CAPTAIN CONNOR'S TEXAS COMPANY OF FOOT.*

Names	Rank	No.	Rank	No.	Miss.	K/W/M	Total
David Campbell,....	1st Lt.,.	1					
John A. Leonard,...	2d Lt., .	1					
Joseph Voot, ...	Corp., .	1					
Edward King, ...	"	2					
James Clark, ...	Private,	1					
Milton P. Donohoe,	"	2					
Michael Donovan, ..	"	3					
Edward Fenney,....	"	4					
Edward Forche, ...	"	5					
Henry Gillerman, ..	"	6					
Emele Godquin, ...	"	7					
James Hays,........	"	8					
Frederick Klinge, ..	"	9					
Caleb Langeson,....	"	10					
John McLean,......	"	11	Private,	1			
	Total, ..	15	....	1	..	16	417
Total in 2d Illinois Regiment and Texas Company,...........		....	62	....	67	2	131	

* Serving with the Second Illinois Regiment.

SECOND INDIANA REGIMENT.

Captain Sanderson's Company A.

Names	Killed. Rank.	No.	Wounded. Rank.	No.	Missing.	Killed, wounded, and miss'g.	Total.
Francis Baily,	Private,	1	Capt.,	1			
Charles H. Goff,	"	2	1st Lt.,	1			
Warren Robinson,	"	3	2d Lt.,	1			
Apollos J. Stevens,	"	4	Priv'ts,	6			
	Total,	4	....	9	..	13	430

Captain Kinder's Company B.

Names	Rank.	No.	Rank.	No.			
T. B. Kinder,	Capt'n,	1					
John T. Hardin,	Private,	1					
Joseph Laffety,	"	2					
Arthur Massey,	"	3					
David McDonald,	"	4	Corp.,	1			
John Shultz,	"	5	Priv'ts,	5			
	Total,	6	....	6	..	12	442

Captain Osborn's Company C.

			Capt.,	1			
			2d Lt.,	1			
			Priv'ts,	8			
				10	..	10	452

Captain Dennis's Company D.

Names	Rank.	No.	Rank.	No.			
Thomas C. Parr,	2d Lt.,	1	Sergt.,	1			
Michael Lee,	Private,	1	Corp.,	1			
Wm. Richardson,	"	2	Musi'n,	1			
James H. Slayden,	"	3	Priv'ts,	5			
	Total,	4		8	..	12	464

Appendix.

Captain Davis's Company **F**.

Killed.			Wounded.		Missing.	Killed, wounded, and miss'g.	Total.
Names.	Rank.	No.	Rank.	No.			
Harvey Matthews,	Private,	1	Sergt.,	2			
Harrison Wilson,	"	2	Corp.,	3			
Ulysses W. Irwin,	"	3	Musi'n,	1			
			Priv'ts,	2			
	Total,	3	....	8	..	11	475

Captain Kimball's Company **G**.

			2d Lt.,	1			
			Sergt.,	2			
			Corp.,	1			
			Priv'ts,	3			
			Total,	7	..	7	482

Captain Briggs's Company **H**.

Meeshack Draper,	Private,	1	Sergt.,	1			
Richard Jenkins,	"	2	Corp.,	1			
Thomas Price,	"	3	Priv'ts,	7			
	Total,	3	....	9	..	12	494

Captain McRae's Company **I**.

John Tager,	Corp.,	1					
Wm. W. Campbell,	Private,	1	Musi'n,	1			
Reuben Harritt,	"	2	Private,	1			
	Total,	3	....	2	1*	6	500

* Private.

APPENDIX. 207

Captain Rousseau's Company E.

Names.	Killed. Rank.	No.	Wounded. Rank.	No.	Missing.	Killed, wounded, and miss'g.	Total.
McHenry Dosier, ..	Sergt., .	1					
Wm. Aikin, ...	Private,	1					
John G. B. Dillon,..	"	2	Priv'ts,	5			
	Total, ..	3	....	5	..	8	508

Captain Walker's Company K.

Names.	Rank.	No.	Rank.	No.	Missing.	K.w.m.	Total.
Wm. Walker, ...	Capt., ..	1					
Alfred Williams,....	Private,	1					
Obadiah Lansbury,..	"	2					
J. C. Higginbotham,	"	3					
Giles Chapman, ...	"	4					
V. Seasely, ...	"	5					
Edmund Wyatt, ...	"	6	2d Lt.,.	1			
Thomas Smith, ...	"	7	Priv'ts,	2			
	Total,..	8	....	3	..	11	519
Total in Second Indiana Regiment,....	....	34	....	67	1	102	

THIRD INDIANA REGIMENT.
Captain Sluss's Company A.

Names.	Rank.	No.	Rank.	No.	Missing.	K.w.m.	Total.
Wm. B. Holland, ..	Private,	1					
James H. Buskirk,..	"	2	Corp., .	1			
David J. Stout,.....	"	3	Priv'ts,	5			
	Total, ..	3	....	6	..	9	528

Captain Allen's Company C.

Names.	Rank.	No.	Rank.	No.	Missing.	K.w.m.	Total.
John Armstrong, ..	Private,	1	Priv'ts,	5	..	6	534

APPENDIX.

Captain Carter's Company **D.**

Killed.			Wounded.		Missing.	Killed, wounded, and miss'g.	Total.
Names.	Rank.	No.	Rank.	No.			
Wilson Houston, ...	Private,	1	Corp., .. Priv'ts,	1 3			
	Total, ..	1	....	4	..	5	539

Captain Taggart's Company **E.**

James Taggart, ...	Capt., ..	1	Corp., .. Priv'ts,	1 3			
	Total, ..	1	....	4	..	5	544

Captain Boardman's Company **F.**

Wm. C. Good, ... Daniel Owens, ...	Private, "	1 2	Corp., .. Priv'ts,	1 7			
	Total, ..	2	....	8	..	10	554

Captain Sullivan's Company **G.**

John A. Graham, ...	Private,	1	Priv'ts,	5	..	6	560

Captain Conover's Company **H.**

			Capt., .. Priv'ts,	1 2			
			Total, .	3	..	3	563

Captain Gibson's Company **I.**

			Private,	1	..	1	564

APPENDIX. 209

CAPTAIN DUNN'S COMPANY K.

KILLED.			WOUNDED.		Missing.	Killed, wounded, and miss'g.	Total.
Names.	Rank.	No.	Rank.	No.			
			Corp.,..	1			
			Priv'ts,	3			
			Total, .	4	..	4	568
Total in Third Indiana Regiment,....	....	9	....	40	..	49	

MISSISSIPPI REGIMENT.
FIELD AND STAFF.

			Colon'l,	1		1	569

CAPTAIN SHARP'S COMPANY A.

William Ingram,....	Sergt., .	1	Capt.,..	1			
C. O'Sullivan, ...	Private,	1	1st Lt.,	1			
			Sergt, .	1			
			Priv'ts,	5			
	Total, ..	2	....	8	..	10	579

CAPTAIN COOPER'S COMPANY B.

Seab. Jones,........	Private,	1					
Thomas H. Titley,..	"	2					
L. Turberville,......	"	3	1st Lt.,	1			
W. H. Wilkinson, ..	"	4	Priv'ts,	5			
	Total, ..	4	....	6	1*	11	590

* Private.

APPENDIX.

Lieutenant Cook's Company C.

Killed.			Wounded.		Missing.	Killed, wounded, and miss'g.	Total.
Names.	Rank.	No.	Rank.	No.			
William Couch, ...	Private,	1					
D. H. Eggleston,....	"	2	Sergt., .	1			
James Johnson, ...	"	3	Corp.,..	4			
John Preston, ...	"	4	Priv'ts,	3			
	Total, ..	4	....	8	..	12	602

Lieutenant Fletcher's Company E.

Killed.			Wounded.		Missing.	Killed, wounded, and miss'g.	Total.
W. W. Phillips, ...	Sergt., .	1					
J. H. Langford,.....	"	2					
F. M. Robinsion,....	Corp.,..	1					
Joseph C. Reville, ..	"	2					
Robert A. Joyce,....	Private,	1					
William Sellers, ...	"	2	Priv'ts,	6			
	Total, ..	6	....	6	..	12	614

Captain Dellay's Company F.

Killed.			Wounded.		Missing.	Killed, wounded, and miss'g.	Total.
B. Higany, ...	Sergt.,..	1					
James H. Blakely,..	Corp., ..	1					
D. L. Butler, ...	"	2					
P. Durivant,........	Private,	1					
Stephen Jones, ...	"	2	Lieut.,.	1			
Enos Garrett, ...	"	3	Priv'ts,	5			
	Total, ..	6	....	6	..	12	626

Captain Downing's Company G.

KILLED.			WOUNDED.		Missing.	Killed, wounded, and miss'g.	Total.
Names.	Rank.	No.	Rank.	No.			
Francis McNulty, ..	2d Lt.,..	1					
J. M. Alexander,....	Corp., ..	1					
James H. Graves,..	Private,	1					
J. S. Bond, ...	"	2					
L. A. Cooper,......	"	3					
W. M. Seay,........	"	4					
Robert Felts, ...	"	5	Corp.,..	3			
Richard E. Parr,....	"	6	Priv'ts,	6			
	Total, ..	8	....	9	..	17	643

Lieutenant Moore's Company H.

R. L. Moore, ...	1st Lt.,.	1					
W. D. Harrison, ...	Private,	1	Sergt.,.	1			
Patrick Rariden,....	"	2	Corp ,..	1			
Jacob Locke, ...	"	3	Priv'ts,	6			
	Total, ..	4	....	8	1*	13	656

Captain Taylor's Company I.

Gar. Anderson,.....	Sergt., .	1					
H. G. Trotter, ...	Private,	1					
J. S. Branch, ...	"	2					
John Pease, ...	"	3					
A. Collingsworth, ..	"	4	Sergt.,.	1			
J. W. Vinson,......	"	5	Priv'ts,	3			
			....				
	Total, ..	6		4	..	10	666
Total in Mississippi Regiment,........	....	40	....	56		98	

* Corporal.

RECAPITULATION.

REGULARS.						
CORPS.	Killed.	Wounded.	Missing.	Aggregate.	Strength went into battle.	Loss, one out of
General Staff, A. A. G. Lincoln,...............	1	..	..	1		
Corps Engineers, ...	..	1	..	1		
3d Artillery, 2 Companies,	1	19	..	20	150	7·5
4th Artillery, 1 Company,	6	22	..	28	117	4·18
1st Dragoons, 2 Companies,	..	9	..	9	133	14·78
2d Dragoons, 2 Companies,	..	2	..	2	76	38
Total of Regulars,........	8	53	..	61	476	

VOLUNTEERS.						
Brigadier-General, (Lane,)	..	1	..	1		
Arkansas Mounted Regiment, (Col. Yell's,)....	18	23	1	42	479	11·4
1st Kentucky Mounted Regiment, (Col. Marshall's,)...............	28	22	..	50	330	6·6
2d Kentucky Foot Regiment, (Col. McKee's,)	44	43	..	87	571	6·56
1st Illinois Foot Regiment, (Col. Hardin's,)	29	16	..	45	580	12·89
2d Illinois Foot Regiment, (Col. Bissell's,)	47	66	2	115	573	4·98
Texas Company, Foot, (Capt. Conner's,)	15	1	..	16	61	3·81
2d Indiana Foot Regiment, (Col. Bowles's,)	34	67	1	102	627	6·13
3d Indiana Foot Regiment, (Col. Lane's,) ..	9	40	..	49	626	12·77
1st Mississippi Foot Regiment, (Col. Davis's,) ..	40	56	2	98	368	3·75
Total of Volunteers,......	264	335	6	605	4,215	
Total of Regulars and Volunteers, ...	272	388	6	666	4,691	

S. CHURCHILL, *Ins. Gen.*

F.
(See page 131.)

Major Mansfield, of the Corps of Engineers, wrote from Agua Nueva, March 1st, a letter, from which the following extracts are made:

"Nothing could exceed the gallant bearing of our horse and dragoons, nor the bravery and good conduct of the volunteers, as a body. Not a regular infantry soldier was in this fight. · · · · ·

"If I had had but one single full regiment of regulars in reserve, we could have charged their battery on our extreme left, and taken 4000 or 5000 prisoners. As it was, we could only hold our own against such odds. · · · · ·

"It was a beautiful battle, — not a mistake made the whole day; but every man perfectly exhausted at night. Our loss about 264 killed, and 450 wounded; the enemy's loss about 2500 in killed and wounded, and 4000 missing."

G.

(See page 142.)

Return of Mexican Prisoners captured at the Battle of Buena Vista, February 22d and 23d, 1847, and subsequently brought in by the Troops under the Command of Major-General Z. Taylor.

Captains.	Lieutenants.	Sub. Lieutenants.	Sergeants.	Corporals.	Musicians.	Privates.	Sappers.	Drivers.	Cooks.	Aggregate.	Remarks.
1	1	1	4	4	4	85	1	4	1	106	Sent from Buena Vista, Feb. 25, in charge of Captain Faulac, to Gen. Santa Anna, for exchange.
						39				39	Fit for duty; confined at Saltillo.
1			5	9		133		1		149	Wounded, and in hospital at Saltillo.
2	1	1	9	13	4	257	1	5	1	294	

S. CHURCHILL,
Inspector-General.

Inspector-General's Department,
Camp at Agua Nueva, March 4, 1847.

H.

(See page 150.)

It will be observed that General Santa Anna claims to have taken "*two* banners" from us, in one of the following letters, and "*three* stands of colors," in the other.

"To General Don Ciriaco Vasquez.

"Agua Nueva, February 25, 1847.

"My esteemed Friend: The haste with which I sent off the last express to the government hindered me from writing to you the news of the deeds of arms. We have fought for two whole days. The enemy awaited us at a point called the Narrows. The battle of the 23d was particularly bloody, on both sides; but it was impossible to take the principal position of the enemy, which is another Thermopylæ, although we drove him from five positions, and took two banners and three guns. The blood ran in torrents, and it is calculated that both armies lost 3000 or 4000 men in killed and wounded. Our bayonet charges resulted in the death of hundreds; but the enemy could not be completely routed, on account of the strong position he occupied. We gave him to understand that the Mexican soldier can fight bravely, breast to breast, and without being deterred, either by strength of position, or by brokenness of ground, or by hunger and thirst, which he suffered with heroic resignation. The strength of the enemy was 9000 men and twenty-six pieces of artillery.

"We have to lament the death of Colonel Berra, Lieutenant-Colonel Anonos, and the commanders of battalions and squadrons, Luyanda, Rios, Peña, besides other officers. General Lombardino, Colonel Brito, Colonel Rocha, General Ángel Guzman, Lieutenant-Colonels Gallozo, Monterdeoca, Andrade, Jicotercal, Ouijano, Basave, Onate, and other chiefs and officers, are wounded.

"I lost my horse by a gunshot in one of the first charges. We are destitute of necessaries for the wounded, and I therefore charge you to send on immediately the provisions in your place, so that they may meet the army, which has done its duty, and saved the honor of the national arms.

"God and Liberty!

"SANTA ANNA."

"To His Excellency, D. Ramon Adame.

"Agua Nueva, February 26, 1847.

"My dear Friend: The hurry in which I wrote my last letter prevented me from sending you a copy of my despatch to the government, and the general order issued to the troops on the field of battle. I now send it, and suppose the triumph of our arms has been celebrated in your town. The want of supplies, together with the dysentery, which broke out in the army, compelled me to listen to the opinions of the generals and chiefs of the army, and regulate my operations accordingly. They unanimously determined that the army ought to fall back on points where supplies might be had. I have, therefore, determined to retire by way of Cedral, Vanegas, and Matahuala, where I can establish a hospital for the wounded, who amount to more than 400, and also for the sick; after which I will return and seek the enemy, provided the government furnishes the necessary resources.

"I have informed the government to this effect, under the present date. I here take occasion to state, as all the world should know it, that the treason of a native Mexican prevented me from gaining a complete victory over our invaders. A soldier from the regiment of cuirassiers, a native of Saltillo, deserted from Encarnacion, and informed General Wool of my approach. General Wool precipitately struck his camp, abandoning a part of his train, and some provisions, and occupied the impregnable position of La Angostura, which it was impossible to reduce, notwithstanding the great advantage gained by our troops, who took five of their positions, three stands of colors, and as many pieces of artillery.

"God and Liberty!

"SANTA ANNA."

I.
(See page 151.)

General Miñon published a letter in the "Independiente," in which, after defending himself, he attempts to account for the disasters of the battle, and denies that the Mexican army was suffering for want of food.

"To the Editors of the 'Independiente.'
"Santa Maria del Rio, April 10, 1847.

"DEAR SIRS : · · · The nation will know, one day, what that was which was called, without shame, the victory of La Angostura; it will know that it had brave soldiers, worthy to rival, in ardor and enthusiasm, the best of any army whatever; that it had intrepid officers, who led them gallantly to the combat, — but that it had no general who knew how to make use of these excellent materials. The nation will know that if, on those memorable fields, a true and splendid victory was not achieved, no one was to blame but him who was charged with leading the forces, because he did not know how to do it. According to the order of the attack, and with a knowledge of the positions occupied by the enemy, speaking in accordance with the rules of art, we ought to have been defeated. We were not, because the valor of our troops overcame all the disadvantages with which we had to struggle. The battle of La Angostura was nothing but an unconnected succession of sublime individual deeds, — partial attacks of the several corps who entered the action. Their chiefs led them according to the divers positions taken by the enemy, in consequence of the partial defeats which he suffered; but there was no methodical direction, no general regulated attack, no plan in which the efforts of the troops, according to their class, were combined, that did, or could, produce a victory. General Santa Anna believes that war is reduced to the fighting of the troops of one and the other party, wherever they meet, and however they choose; General Santa Anna believes that a battle is no more than the shock of men, with much noise, shouts, and shots, to see who can do the most, each in his own way; General Santa Anna cannot conceive how it happens that a victory may be gained over an enemy by wise and well-calculated manœuvres. Thus it is, that he has everywhere been routed, and he always will be, unless he should have the fortune to meet with one who has the same ideas with himself in relation to war.

"But, leaving it to others to elucidate all that happened during this campaign of February, the very grave faults committed by the general who conducted it, and the fatal consequences which it immediately had, and which it will continue to have, on the war in which we are engaged, I shall confine myself to that which concerns me. It is false that I was not present at the rear-guard of the enemy during the battle of the 23d of February. I was not only present, but I suffered, with the whole brigade which I commanded, from the fire they kept up on us. The whole city of Saltillo, in sight of which I was all day, and the enemy himself, will testify to it. · · · · We were so much present, that General Taylor ordered six pieces of artillery to open upon us at that point, and there were more than a thousand men engaged in observing my brigade, who took no part in the action;— these lessened the force that General Santa Anna had to fight. I did not withdraw from there till nightfall, and when the battle had entirely ceased. I retired within view of the enemy's troops, who sallied from Saltillo, with four pieces of cannon, to engage us. The roughness of the ground,— wholly cut up by an infinity of deep ravines,— rendered useless any attempt whatever on the part of my cavalry. · · ·

"*The only reason, the true cause*, of this animosity of General Santa Anna towards me, is, that I disapproved of his retiring from the field of Angostura, as is seen by my communications, numbered 4 and 5. I believed then, and I believe now, that the army which had left San Luis might have remained at that point, and completed the great work, which it had undertaken, of destroying the enemy. Many believe the same as I do. It is false that there was not food or water. There was every thing,—I myself supplied General Santa Anna. I advised him repeatedly of what I had at my disposition,—beeves, corn, flour,—where I was. I indicated to him the route by which he could move, without embarrassment, to Saltillo, without scarcity of water, of forage for the horses, or of provisions for the troops. I had not less than 700 beeves confined in an enclosure, all of which I shared with him as opportunity offered. His retirement was unjustifiable, and much more so from the manner in which he undertook it,—in the midst of the darkness of night,—abandoning, without necessity, hundreds of the unhappy wounded, and, in appearance, much more like that of a fugitive, desirous of concealing from the enemy his defeat, that he might not finish his destruction, than that of a general who desired to take breathing-time, but who could have obliged any that attempted to impede him to give way. This is the *only and true cause* of my persecution,—there is no other. General Santa Anna properly supposed that I would not desist from speaking, and telling the nation what had occurred on those days, and he desired to prevent me. He imprisoned me, and cut me off from all communication. He desired, at the same time, to deprive me of my papers, in order to make my vindication impossible; but I preserved them, thanks to my foresight, and will answer, with dates, whatever charges they may bring against me. If there is any thing painful to me in this affair, it is that I am withdrawn from the front of the enemy, and deprived of the privilege of shedding my blood for my country, to which I owe all, — my rank and my subsistence. This I feel, — nothing else. May I be permitted to give my feeble services, to pay, in some manner, this sacred debt; I will do it to merit my country's esteem; and if I enjoy that, of no consequence to me is the hatred of my enemies, whom I pity and despise.

"J. V. MIÑON."

J.
(See page 155.)

The following extract of a letter, dated March 22, 1847, from the Secretary of War to General Scott, indicates the extreme solicitude which was felt at Washington, at General Taylor's critical condition; and, also, the just appreciation which the Department of War entertained of the momentous consequences depending on the battle:

" The information which has just reached us in the shape of rumors, as to the situation of General Taylor, and the forces under his command, has excited the most painful apprehensions for his safety. It is almost certain that Santa Anna has precipitated the large army he had collected at San Luis de Potosí upon General Taylor; and it may be, that the General has not been able to maintain the advanced position he had seen fit to take at Agua Nueva, but has been obliged to fall back on Monterey. It is equally certain, that a Mexican force has been interposed between Monterey and the Rio Grande, and that it has interrupted the line of communication between the two places, and seized large supplies, which were on their way to General Taylor's army.

"If the hostile force between the Rio Grande and General Taylor's army is as large as report represents it, our troops now on that river may not be able to reëstablish the line; nor will it, perhaps, be possible to place a force there, sufficient for the purpose, in time to prevent disastrous consequences to our army, *unless aid can be afforded from the troops under your immediate command.*

"From one to two thousand of the new recruits for the ten regiments, from this quarter, will be on the way to the Brazos, in the course of three or four days. All the other forces will be directed to that point, and every effort made to relieve General Taylor from his critical situation. You will have been fully apprized, before this can reach you, of the condition of things in the Valley of the Rio Grande, and at the headquarters of General Taylor; and have taken, I trust, such measures as the importance of the subject requires. I need not urge upon you the fatal consequences which would result from any serious disaster which might befall the army under General Taylor, nor do I doubt that you will do what is in your power to avert such a calamity."

K.

These are the orders issued to the troops after the battle of Buena Vista:

"Head-Quarters, Army of Occupation,
Buena Vista, February 26, 1847.

"The commanding General has the grateful task of congratulating the troops upon the brilliant success which attended their arms in the conflict of the 22d and 23d. Confident in their superiority of numbers, and stimulated by the presence of a distinguished leader, the Mexican troops were yet repulsed in every effort to force our lines, and finally withdrew, with immense loss, from the field.

"The General would express his obligations to the officers and men engaged, for the cordial support which they rendered throughout the action; it will be his highest pride to bring to the notice of the government the conspicuous gallantry of particular officers and corps, whose unwavering steadiness more than once saved the fortunes of the day. He would also express his high satisfaction with the conduct of a small command left to hold Saltillo; though not so seriously engaged as their comrades, their services were very important and efficiently rendered. While bestowing this just tribute to the good conduct of the troops, the General deeply regrets to say that there were a few exceptions. He trusts that those who fled ingloriously from Buena Vista, and went to Saltillo, will seek an opportunity to retrieve their reputation, and to emulate the bravery of their comrades, who bore the brunt of the battle, and sustained, against fearful odds, the honor of the flag. The exultation of success is checked by the heavy sacrifice of life which it has cost, embracing many officers of high rank and high merit. While the sympathies of a grateful country will be given to the bereaved families and friends of those who nobly fell, their illustrious example will remain for the benefit and admiration of the army.

"By order of General Taylor.

"W. W. S. BLISS,
"Assistant Adjutant-General."

L.

General Orders, No. 54.

Head-Quarters of the Army of the U. S.,
Vergara, before Vera Cruz, March 15, 1847.

The General-in-Chief of the army has received authentic information of a great and glorious victory, obtained by the arms of our country under the successful Major-General Taylor, at Buena Vista, near Saltillo, on the 22d and 23d ultimo. The general results were 4000 of the enemy killed and wounded, against our loss of 700 gallant men. General Santa

Anna, on sustaining that overwhelming defeat, is known to have retreated upon San Louis de Potosí, and probably will not stop short of the capital.

The General-in-Chief imparts this glorious news to the army, that all with him may participate in the joy that is now spreading itself throughout the breadth of our country.

By command of Major-General Scott.

H. L. SCOTT, *A. A. A. G.*

No official report is yet received.

WINFIELD SCOTT.

March 17, 1847.

M.

WAR DEPARTMENT,
April 3, 1847.

SIR: Your communications of the 24th and 25th of February and the 1st of March, announcing the brilliant success of the troops under your command at Buena Vista, against the forces of the enemy vastly superior in numbers, have been laid before the President, and I am instructed to convey to you his high appreciation of the distinguished services rendered to the country by yourself and the officers and soldiers of your command on that occasion.

The victory achieved at Buena Vista, while it adds new glory to our arms, and furnishes new proofs of the valor and brave daring of our officers and soldiers, will excite the admiration and call forth the gratitude of the nation.

The single fact that 5000 of our troops, nearly all volunteers, who, yielding to the impulse of patriotism, had rallied to their country's standard for a temporary service, were brought into conflict with an army of 20,000, mostly veteran soldiers, and not only stood and repulsed the assaults of this numerous host, led by their most experienced general, but in a protracted battle of two days won a glorious victory, is the most indubitable evidence of the consummate skill and gallant conduct of our officers and the devoted heroism of the troops under their command. It will ever be a proud distinction to have been in the memorable battle of *Buena Vista*.

The general joy which the intelligence of this success of our arms has spread through the land is mingled with regret that it has been obtained at so great a price, — that so many heroic men have fallen in that sanguinary conflict. They died in the intrepid discharge of a patriotic duty, and will be honored and lamented by a grateful nation.

You will cause this communication to be published to the troops under your command.

I have the honor to be,

Very respectfully, your ob't serv't,

W. L. MARCY,
Secretary of War.

To Major-General Z. TAYLOR.

N.

On the 28th of January, Santa Anna issued this proclamation to his army, and directed that it should be read at the head of every regiment, and that a printed copy be furnished to each company.

"His Excellency the General-in-Chief of the Army of Operations of the North, to all under his command.

"COMPANIONS IN ARMS! The operations of the enemy require of us to move precipitately on their principal line; and we are about to do it. The independence, the honor, and the destinies of the nation depend, in this movement, on your decision.

" Soldiers! The entire world is observing us; and it is obligatory on you that your deeds should be as heroic as they are necessary, from the neglect and abandonment with which you have been treated by those whose duty it is to succor you. Privations of all kinds await you; but when has want or penury weakened your spirit or debilitated your enthusiasm? The Mexican soldier is well known for his frugality and his capability of sufferance. Never does he need magazines of provisions when about to pass the deserts; but he has always had an eye to the resources and supplies of his enemy to administer to his own wants. To-day you commence your march, through a thinly-settled country, without supplies and without provisions; but you may be assured that very quickly you will be in possession of those of your enemy, and of his riches; and with them all your wants will be superabundantly remedied.

"My friends! We are about to open the campaign; and who can tell us how many days of glory await us! What a perspective, so full of hope for our country! What satisfaction will you feel, when you contemplate that you have saved our independence! that you are the objects of admiration to the whole world, and that our own country will shower down blessings on your head! O, when again in the bosoms of your families you shall relate your dangers and hardships suffered, your combats and triumphs over your daring, presumptuous foe, — when you tell your children that *you* have given them their country a second time, — your jubilee will be complete; and how insignificant will your sacrifices appear!

"Soldiers! Trust confidingly in the destinies of your country. The cause we sustain is *holy*, and never have we gone to the conflict with so much justice, for we are defending the home of our forefathers and of our posterity, — our honor, — our holy religion, — our wives, — our children. What sacrifice is too great for objects so dear? Let our motto be, "To conquer or die." Let us swear before the Eternal, that we will not rest one instant until we completely wipe away from our soil the vain-glorious foreigner who has dared to pollute it with his presence. No terms with him, — nothing for us but heroism and grandeur.

"ANTONIO LOPEZ DE SANTA ANNA.
"Head-Quarters, in San Luis Potosí, Jan. 27, 1847.
"By order of his Excellency.
"MICHELTORENA."

APPENDIX. 229

O.

This is the order of march commencing the movement of the "LIBERATING ARMY OF THE NORTH" from San Luis de Potosí.

"GENERAL ORDERS, JAN. 26, 1847.

"*Officer-in-Chief of the Day* — LIEUTENANT-COLONEL DON MANUEL ROMERO.

"*Head-Quarters 1st Brigade.* — *Order of march of the Army.*

"By general order, the General-in-Chief commands that the baggage shall not be carried with the army, nor shall the soldiers take their knapsacks, but shall wear their dress of Russia duck, and over this their suit of cloth; they shall only take two shirts, four rounds of cartridges, and two flints, including the one in their guns; they shall carry nothing except their cooking utensils. All the officers and other persons shall march in their places, and, when bivouacking, shall keep at the head of their respective commands.

"On the 27th, the following pieces of artillery will march: Three 24's, three 16's, five 12's, and eight 8-pounders, and one howitzer, with ammunition corresponding to each, and also the platforms for the large pieces; 500 boxes of musket-ammunition, 12,000 flints, and the remainder of the canister and grape of the three pieces, which were in Tula, — all of which will be placed in the twenty-one wagons contracted for; and what remains, on 450 mules, which the chief of the staff will order to be delivered to the commanding officer of artillery. The ammunition of the pieces above expressed will be escorted by themselves, and by the company of sappers and miners who belong to the regiment of engineers, and by the artillerists of the light brigade, who will take with them all the implements necessary for sapping and mining, in the wagons which the sappers have; the sacks for filling with earth will be carried on mules, which will be furnished by the chief of the staff.

"On Thursday, the 28th, the 5th brigade of infantry, under the command of Don Francisco Pacheco, will commence its march, sending ahead always, the evening previous, an officer to procure lodgings and prepare rations for the troops.

"On Friday, the 29th, the 1st and 2d brigades will march out in the same manner, under the orders of Don Rafael Garcia Conde; these brigades will be considered as united until further orders, and consequently all the infantry is placed under the command of General of Brigade, Don Manuel Maria Lombardini.

"On Saturday, the 30th, the 4th and 6th brigades will march in like manner, under the command of Brigadier-General Don Luis Guzman.

"The medical staff having left in the hospitals of this city four junior surgeons, and only the necessaries for the service, all the rest will march, apportioned among the different brigades, under the orders of the Medical Inspector-General, with all their medicines, and articles necessary for the campaign.

"The General's staff and its chief will depart, after having advanced all the brigades and material of war, taking particular care that, after arriving at Matahuala, the staff will be distributed to each division, according to the necessities of the service.

"All the military left in the city will know as their Commander-in-Chief the General of Brigade, Don Juan Amador, under whose command are the fortifications, instruction, and discipline of the troops, and likewise the defence of the city and state, — he being the commanding General. There will remain in this city only those soldiers who are incapable of doing service in the campaign. And on the morning of the 29th, they, — all the new recruits, — the sick, the weak, and unarmed, will be marched in and take possession of the different barracks; for it is the desire of the President General-in-Chief, that only those soldiers should march who are capable of performing the duties and bearing the fatigues and privations of war.

"Each brigade will leave in this city persons capable of instructing their recruits; and, for the defence of the place, at least one captain, and subalterns in proportion to their respective numbers.

"The General-in-Chief, Don Manuel Maria Lombardini, will order that, by twelve o'clock, A. M., tomorrow, a list be made and delivered to the chief of the staff, of all the baggage to be transported belonging to each and every corps. The artillery, engineer, quartermaster, and medical staffs will also comply with this order.

"The chief of the staff will remit to each chief of section instructions necessary for the march.

"Every officer belonging to this army, whatever may be his rank or title, will read to the troops under his command the following order:

"1st. Any person who may desert his flag shall suffer *death*, agreeably to article 57th, of the 29th December, 1838.

"2d. Any person who may be found half a league distant from this city, or from the camp, shall be considered guilty of the crime of *desertion*.

"By order of his Excellency,

"SALAZAR, *Colonel*,
"VASQUEZ, *General of Brigade.*"

P.

This is the final order of march and general disposition of the Mexican army on leaving La Encarnacion for Agua Nueva. Many important discrepancies exist between it and Santa Anna's Report, made out *after* the Battle of Buena Vista.

"GENERAL ORDERS OF THE 20TH AND THE 21ST FEB. 1847.

"*General Officer of the Day* — DON RAFAEL VASQUEZ.

"*Aides* — COL. JOSÉ MA. BERMUDEA, AND LIEUT.-COL. DON FLORENCIO ASPEITIA.

"*And for to-morrow* — DON FRANCISCO MEJIA, *General Officer of the Day.*

"*Aides* — Col. Don Carlos Brito, and Lieut.-Col. Don Gregorio Elati.

"In the morning the army will continue its march, which will commence at eleven o'clock precisely, in the following order:

"The 1st, 2d, 3d, and 4th battalions of light infantry will take the lead, under the orders of General Ampudia, so that he may be able to avail himself of all advantages that the circumstances may require; immediately after, the battalion of sappers; and in its rear, and at the head of the division of infantry of the van, under the orders of General Pacheco, will be placed the company of sharp-shooters, and three pieces of 16's, with their respective artillerists and reserve; as likewise the ammunition, composed of 100 round shot and 100 grape for each piece, and 80 boxes of musket ammunition, each containing 9600 cartridges.

"Division of infantry of the centre, commanded by General Manuel Ma. Lombardini, will follow. At the head of this column there will be five 12's, as above named and ammunitioned, and also 80 boxes of musket ammunition.

"At the head of the division of the rear, commanded by General Ortega, there will be five pieces of 8's, supplied with men and ammunition as above, and also its 80 boxes of musket ammunition, each containing 9600 cartridges.

"The division of cavalry of the rear will follow closely on the last of infantry, having at their head the hussars, and in their rear the general ammunition train, escorted by the brigade of horse artillery; after the ammunition train, all the camp followers of all classes, with the baggage of all kinds, laundresses, cooks, &c., — it being distinctly understood that no woman will be allowed to mix with the column. The chief in charge of the commissary department is Don Pedro Rangel, who is also in charge of the baggage train.

"His Excellency, the General-in-Chief, furthermore orders that the different corps shall to-day receive from the commissary three days' rations,* for the 21st, 22d, and 23d; and that they require the necessary meat this afternoon for the first meal to-morrow morning, which the troops are directed to eat one hour before taking up the line of march; and the second will be taken in their haversacks, to be eaten in the night, wherever they may halt; this last will consist of meat, two biscuits, and half a cake of (*piloncillo*) brown sugar for each man; for, on the night of the 21st there will be no fires permitted, neither will signal be made by any military instrument of music, the movement at early daybreak on the morning of the 22d having to be made in the most profound silence.

"The troops will drink all the water they can before marching, and will take with them in their canteens, or other vessels, all they can possibly carry; they will economize the water all they can, for we shall encamp at night without water, and shall not arrive at it until the following day. The chief of corps will pay *much, much, much* attention to this last instruction.

"Each mule belonging to the ammunition train, and the horses of officers, will receive two rations of corn, which they will take with them; and these will be fed to them to-morrow night at dusk; and

---

* See the extract from Santa Anna's letter to the Minister of War and Marine on page 151, in which he says his troops had but *one* ration.

on the following morning, at daybreak, the horses' girths will only be slackened, and the mules will not be unharnessed while they are eating. The light brigade will likewise obey this order on the night of the 21st, only loosening their saddles a little. The horses and mules will all be taken to water before commencing the march.

"Each division will take with it its respective medical staff, hospital attendants, medicines, &c., as regulated by the Medical Inspector-General.

"The chaplain-in-chief will provide each division with its chaplain. He will also, as to-morrow is a feast day, order mass to be said at six o'clock in front of the position occupied by the vanguard, at seven o'clock in front of the centre, at eight o'clock in front of the rear guard, and at nine o'clock in front of the division of cavalry.

"General Don Francisco Perez is ordered to be recognized as second in command to General Lombardini, and General Don Luis Guzman as second to General Ortega.

"To facilitate the duties of the conductor-general of the baggage train, the cavalry of Celaya and all the presidial troops are hereby placed under his command.

"His Excellency, the General-in-Chief, recommends to every officer punctual compliance with, and obedience to, each and every part of this, his general order.

"By order of his Excellency,

"MANUEL MICHELTORENA,

"*Chief of the General Staff.*"

Q.

The following is a list of the officers still in the Regular Army, who were engaged in the operations referred to in the foregoing narrative. Their *present* rank is prefixed to their names, and they are placed in the position they *now* occupy, whether in the Staff or in the Line.

GENERAL OFFICERS.

Major-General ZACHARY TAYLOR,
Brevet Major-General JOHN E. WOOL.

GENERAL STAFF.

ADJUTANT-GENERAL'S DEPARTMENT.

Brevet Lieutenant-Colonel William W. S. Bliss,
Brevet Captain Irvin McDowell.

INSPECTOR-GENERAL'S DEPARTMENT.

Brevet Brigadier-General Sylvester Churchill.

QUARTERMASTER'S DEPARTMENT.

Colonel Henry Whiting,
Brevet Major Ebenezer S. Sibley,
Brevet Major William W. Chapman,
Brevet Major James L. Donaldson.

SUBSISTENCE DEPARTMENT.

Brevet Major Amos B. Eaton.

MEDICAL DEPARTMENT.

Surgeon Presley H. Craig,
Assistant Surgeon Charles M. Hitchcock,
Assistant Surgeon Thomas C. Madison,
Assistant Surgeon William Levely,
Assistant Surgeon Grayson M. Prevost.

APPENDIX. 237

PAY DEPARTMENT.

Brevet Lieutenant-Colonel ROGER S. DIX,
Major ANDREW J. COFFEE.

CORPS OF ENGINEERS.

Brevet Colonel JOSEPH K. F. MANSFIELD,
Brevet Captain HENRY W. BENHAM.

CORPS OF TOPOGRAPHICAL ENGINEERS.

Brevet Major THOMAS B. LINNARD,
Brevet Captain LORENZO SITGREAVES,
Brevet Captain JOHN POPE,
Brevet 1st Lieutenant WILLIAM B. FRANKLIN,
Brevet 1st Lieutenant FRANCIS T. BRYAN.

ORDNANCE DEPARTMENT.

Brevet Lieutenant-Colonel HENRY K. CRAIG,
Brevet 1st Lieutenant CHARLES P. KINGSBURY.

LINE.

FIRST REGIMENT OF DRAGOONS.

Captain ENOCH STEEN,
Captain ROBERT H. CHILTON,
Captain DANIEL H. RUCKER,
Captain JAMES H. CARLETON,
1st Lieutenant ABRAHAM BUFORD,
1st Lieutenant JOSEPH H. WHITTLESEY,
2d Lieutenant SAMUEL D. STURGIS,
2d Lieutenant GEORGE F. EVANS.

SECOND REGIMENT OF DRAGOONS.

Brevet Lieutenant-Colonel CHARLES A. MAY,
1st Lieutenant REUBEN P. CAMPBELL,
2d Lieutenant NEWTON C. GIVENS,
2d Lieutenant THOMAS J. WOOD.

FIRST REGIMENT OF ARTILLERY.

Brevet Major LUCIAN B. WEBSTER,
Captain JAMES H. PRENTISS,
1st Lieutenant JAMES B. RICKETTS,
1st Lieutenant ISAAC BOWEN,
1st Lieutenant ABNER DOUBLEDAY.

SECOND REGIMENT OF ARTILLERY.

Brevet Colonel JOHN MUNROE.

THIRD REGIMENT OF ARTILLERY.

Brevet Lieutenant-Colonel BRAXTON BRAGG,
Brevet Lieutenant-Colonel JOHN M. WASHINGTON,
Brevet Major THOMAS W. SHERMAN,
Brevet Major WILLIAM H. SHOVER,
Brevet Major GEORGE H. THOMAS,
Brevet Captain JOHN F. REYNOLDS,
Brevet Captain SAMUEL G. FRENCH.

FOURTH REGIMENT OF ARTILLERY.

Brevet Major ROBERT S. GARNETT,
Brevet Major JOHN P. J. O'BRIEN,
Brevet Captain THOMAS L. BRENT,
1st Lieutenant HENRY M. WHITING,
1st Lieutenant DARIUS N. COUCH.

THIRD REGIMENT OF INFANTRY.

Brevet Major JOSEPH H. EATON.

FIFTH REGIMENT OF INFANTRY.

Brevet Colonel WILLIAM G. BELKNAP.

THE END.

THE NAVAL & MILITARY PRESS
Specialist Books For The Serious Student Of Conflict

Military book enthusiasts now have a place on the internet dedicated to themselves. Our site is the most extensive devoted to military history on the web. You can browse and shop through our vast range of titles by time period or by theme, or use our advanced search facilities to find areas of specific interest.

The Naval & Military Press Ltd was founded in 1991 and quickly established itself as a mecca for the military enthusiast. Over 35,000 customers worldwide enjoy receiving our booklist which contains many hundreds of first-class books. With the advances in technology we are now pleased to show all of you with access to the internet our full catalogue. Updated regularly, you can count on the same level of service that our existing customers enjoy.

Our own publications feature strongly on both our list and our website. The innovative approach we have to military bookselling and our commitment to publishing have made us Britain's leading independent military bookseller.

Many titles featured on this website are not unavailable through any other source in the world.

www.naval-military-press.com

General Sir Ian Hamilton's
Staff Officer's Scrap-Book during the Russo–Japanese War
1904–1905
9781474538077

As Hamilton was the military attaché of the British Indian Army serving with the Japanese army in Manchuria during the Russo-Japanese War, he was well placed to publish in 1907 this impressive eye witness account to a military confrontation between a well-known European army and a less-familiar Asian army. Good maps (many in colour), a full index and 600+ pages make this facsimile two-volume set a fine reference for the modern scholar, of a war that is still the classic example of a conflict waged for purely imperialistic motives, a rivalry for the control of Korea and Manchuria and indeed for the mastery of the Far East and China.

The Golden Chersonese and the way thither
9781905748198

A delightful description of her travels in Malaya and China in the 1880s by that intrepid lady Isabella L. Bird, first female member of the Royal Geographical Society and doyenne of all women travel writers.

NOTES FROM A JOURNAL OF RESEARCH INTO THE NATURAL HISTORY OF THE COUNTRIES VISITED DURING THE VOYAGE OF H.M.S. SAMARANG under the command of Captain Sir Edward Belcher, C.B., F.R.A.S.
9781905748013

Like Darwin on the Beagle, surgeon Arthur Adams was a naturalist with this 1843-45 Naval expedition to Japan and the Indian and China Seas. Contains fascinating descriptions of the region's flora and fauna.

LOW`S HISTORY of the INDIAN NAVY
9781474536530

This is an extremely rare work, in its original edition, and covers the life span of the Indian Navy, 1600 to 1863. Operations from the Persian Gulf to the Burma and First China Wars, from Aden to New Zealand and the Maori Wars, and the Indian Mutiny. Survey work from the Red Sea to the China Seas.

NARRATIVE OF THE EARL OF ELGIN'S MISSION TO CHINA AND JAPAN IN THE YEARS 1857, '58, '59
9781905748051

Superbly illustrated two-volume account of Lord Elgin's expeditions to the Far East in 1857-59 which resulted in the occupation of Canton, the burning of Peking's Imperial Summer Palace; and the opening of Japan to European trade.

"CHINA JIM" Being Incidents and Adventures in the Life of an Indian Mutiny Veteran
9781845748463

An account of the author's experiences in the Indian Mutiny and the Second China War. The author acquired his nickname as a result of the immense amount of loot he acquired from the Summer Palace at Peking!

CHINESE WAR, AN ACCOUNT OF ALL THE OPERATIONS OF THE BRITISH FORCES 1842
9781843428176

Detailed account of the first Chinese 'Opium war' with Britain. With 53 fascinating illustrations.

VOYAGE OF HIS MAJESTY'S SHIP ALCESTE, to China, Corea, and the Island of Lewchew, with an account of her shipwreck
9781905748068

Rather aptly summed up by the title, this book was written by the ship's surgeon on the 'Alceste' which was charged with delivering the British Embassy of Lord Amherst to China in 1816. Passing through Rio de Janeiro, the Cape of Good Hope and Batavia en-route, they arrived in the China Sea in the summer and their first meetings with the Chinese together with some of the politics of the time are described here.

OFFICIAL ACCOUNT OF THE MILITARY OPERATIONS IN CHINA 1900-1901
9781783311156

This official account of the military operations in China at the time of the Boxer Rebellion and the siege of the Foreign Legations in Peking was originally compiled by Major Norrie, a member of the Intelligence Staff of the British Contingent, China Field Force. It was considerably revised, edited and expanded by the Intelligence Department at the War Office. It begins with the rise of the Boxer Secret Society and the outbreak of hostilities against foreigners in the northern provinces, extends to cover the operations for the relief of Foreign Legations in Peking and concludes with the peace negotiations and withdrawal of the greater part of the allied forces from China, original editions are excessively rare.

THE CRUISE OF THE PEARL WITH AN ACCOUNT OF THE OPERATIONS OF THE NAVAL BRIGADE IN INDIA
9781843428206

Drawn from the unusual diary of a naval Chaplain detailing the exploits of a scratch Naval Brigade, consisting of warship crews fighting on shore, in quelling the Indian Mutiny in 1857-58. Charming, despite the grim nature of much of the material.

THE LAST CRUISE OF THE "MAJESTIC"
George Goodchild from the log book of Petty Officer J.G. Cowie
9781474539166

Interesting personal account of the service of battleship "Majestic" in the Dardanelles arranged by Goodchild from the logbook of Petty Officer J.G. Cowie. "Majestic" was a Majestic-class pre-dreadnought battleship. In early 1915, she was dispatched to the Mediterranean for service in the Dardanelles Campaign. She participated in bombardments of Turkish forts and supported the Allied landings at Gallipoli. On 27 May 1915, she was torpedoed by the German submarine U-21 at Cape Helles, sinking with the loss of 49 men.

THE COMMISSION OF HMS TERRIBLE 1898-1902
9781843425533

Naval Brigades in South African War & China 1900. Various nominal rolls.

THE NAVAL BRIGADE IN SOUTH AFRICA DURING THE YEARS 1877-78-79
9781843429203

An account of the actions of the Naval Brigade from 'HMS Active' in South Africa's Kaffir and Zulu wars in 1877-79. Written by the Brigade's principal medical officer.

THE HISTORY OF THE BALTIC CAMPAIGN OF 1854, FROM DOCUMENTS AND OTHER MATERIALS FURNISHED BY VICE-ADMIRAL SIR C. NAPIER
9781845742126

A full history of the Crimean War's 'forgotten' sideshow in the Baltic, based on the papers of the British Commander, Admiral Napier, which exonerates him from charges of incompetence.

www.ingramcontent.com/pod-product-compliance
Lightning Source LLC
Chambersburg PA
CBHW060115170426
43198CB00010B/900